C

Korean
phrasebook

Consultant
Jaehoon Yeon

First published 2007
Copyright © HarperCollins Publishers
Reprint 10 9 8 7 6 5 4 3 2 1 0
Typeset by Davidson Pre-Press, Glasgow
Printed in Malaysia by Imago

www.collins.co.uk

ISBN 13 978-0-00-7246809
ISBN 10 0-00-724680-3

Using your phrasebook

Your *Collins Gem Phrasebook* is designed to help you locate the exact phrase you need, when you need it, whether on holiday or for business. If you want to adapt the phrases, you can easily see where to substitute your own words using the dictionary section, and the clear, full-colour layout gives you direct access to the different topics.

The Gem Phrasebook includes:

- Over 70 topics arranged thematically. Each phrase is accompanied by a simple pronunciation guide which eliminates any problems pronouncing foreign words.

- A top ten tips section to safeguard against any cultural faux pas, giving essential dos and don'ts for situations involving local customs or etiquette.

- Practical hints to make your stay trouble free, showing you where to go and what to do when dealing with everyday matters such as travel or hotels and offering valuable tourist information.

- Face to face sections so that you understand what is being said to you. These example mini-dialogues give you a good idea of what to expect from a real conversation.

3

- Common announcements and messages you may hear, ensuring that you never miss the important information you need to know when out and about.

- A clearly laid-out dictionary means you will never be stuck for words.

- A basic grammar section which will enable you to build on your phrases.

- A list of public holidays to avoid being caught out by unexpected opening and closing hours, and to make sure you don't miss the celebrations!

It's worth spending time before you embark on your travels just looking through the topics to see what is covered and becoming familiar with what might be said to you.

Whatever the situation, your *Gem Phrasebook* is sure to help!

Contents

Pronouncing Korean

The Korean alphabet, Hangul, was devised by King Sejong and was promulgated in 1446 during his reign. Before Hangul was devised, there was no adequate way of depicting the Korean language in written form. The only method available was through the use of Chinese characters. However, Korean and Chinese are unrelated languages, and because of this the system was completely unsatisfactory. Hangul is a simple and scientific writing system, and it is easy to learn. Koreans are proud of Hangul, and October 9 is celebrated as **Hangul Day** in Korea.

This phrasebook gives you a romanized version of the Korean alphabet. This is not because the Korean alphabet is unimportant or difficult to learn, but because most people want to know how to pronounce the Korean quickly, and the easiest way to do this is with the romanization.

There are several different methods of romanizing Korean, and the one used in this book is a modified and simplified version of what is known as the McCune-Reischauer system.

Consonants

Pronouncing Korean

letter	approximate pronunciation	symbol
ㄱ	**k** as in **k**ey	k
ㄲ	tensed **k** as in s**k**y	kk
ㄴ	**n** as in **n**o	n
ㄷ	**t** as in **t**in	t
ㄸ	tensed **t** as in s**t**ar	tt
ㄹ	between English **r** and **l**	r/l
ㅁ	**m** as in **m**oon	m
ㅂ	**p** as in **p**ark	p
ㅃ	tensed **p** as in s**p**a	pp
ㅅ	**s** as in **s**un, except before an '**i**' or '**ee**' sound when it is pronounced like the **sh** in **sh**ip or **sh**eep	s/sh
ㅆ	tensed **s** as in **s**ip	ss
ㅇ	zero or null consonant in initial position **ng** as in si**ng** in final position	ng
ㅈ	**ch** as in **ch**arm	ch
ㅉ	tensed **ch** as in **j**azz	cch
ㅊ	aspirated **ch**	ch'
ㅋ	aspirated **k**	k'
ㅌ	aspirated **t**	t'
ㅍ	aspirated **p**	p'
ㅎ	**h** as in **h**ello	h

Vowels

letter	approximate pronunciation	symbol
ㅏ	**a** as in **a**rm	a
ㅑ	**ya** as in **ya**rd	ya
ㅓ	**u** as in f**u**r	ŏ
ㅕ	**yea** as in **yea**rn	yŏ
ㅗ	**aw** as in l**aw**	o
ㅛ	**yo** as in **yo**ga	yo
ㅜ	**oo** as in b**oo**t	oo
ㅠ	**you** as in **you**	yoo
ㅡ	**u** as in b**u**rn	u
ㅣ	**ee** as in f**ee**t	i
ㅔ	**e** as in b**e**d	e
ㅐ	**a** as in b**a**d	ae

There are a number of points to note:

k, **t**, **p** and **ch** are all written as such at the beginning of a word; however, in actual pronunciation, they can be pronounced **g**, **d**, **b** and **j** if they are preceded and followed by vowel sounds. This is not indicated in the romanization, so they can be pronounced in slightly different ways. Note that the distinction between **k**, **t**, **p**, **ch** and **g**, **d**, **b**, **j**

9

is not important. However, in the middle of a word, these letters **k**, **t**, **p**, **ch** are written as **g**, **d**, **b** and **j** when they occur between vowels. Therefore, the word which is written in Korean letters as **hako** will be romanized here as **hago**.

The consonants **m** and **n** are romanized as **m** and **n**; double consonants are written as **kk**, **tt**, **pp**, **cch**; aspirated consonants are written as **k'**, **t'**, **p'**, **ch'**; and the zero or null consonant is not romanized since it has no sound. Remember, however, to write the zero/null consonant in the Korean script when a syllable begins with a vowel. If the zero/null consonant appears as the last consonant in a syllable, it is romanized as **ng**, which is the way it is pronounced (as in bri**ng**).

The letter **h** is sometimes not pronounced; in those cases it is not romanized, although its presence is sometimes indicated in brackets, as in the word **man(h)i**, pronounced **mani**. When the letter **h** occurs as the last consonant in a syllable and the following syllable begins with **k**, **t**, **p** or **ch**, those sounds become aspirated. Instead of writing **hk** in the romanization, it is therefore written **k'**, which is the way the Korean is actually pronounced.

The consonant **s** is pronounced **sh** (as in **sh**all) when it is followed by the vowel **i**, and it is romanized as **sh** in such instances. Note that **ss**+**i** is pronounced **shi**, but is romanized as **ssi**.

Finally, the consonant **l** is a litte tricky. Sometimes it is pronounced **l** (when one of the letters to the side of it is a consonant), but between vowels it is pronounced **r**. It is romanized as **l** or **r** according to the pronunciation of the particular word. Take the word **il**, for example, which means day. When the word is followed by the subject particle -**i**, the **l** is pronounced as an **r**, so it is romanized as **ir-i**. It sounds a bit puzzling at first, but you will soon get used to it, and there is no real difficulty.

The vowels are straightforward, and are romanized in the way described in the Korean alphabet section at the beginning of the book. Be careful to look out for the two **o's' o** and **ŏ**, however, as the distinction between the two is not indicated. Both are romanized as **o**, in case the distinction is not so great that it makes any difference to the meaning. Also remember that **u** is pronounced as the **u** in b**u**rn; **oo** is pronounced as the **u** in l**u**te.

In conclusion, a word about double consonants. This means two syllables in which the first ends with the same consonant as the initial consonant in the second (**om-ma**; **man-na**; **hal-la**). In these cases, hold on to the consonant sound a little longer than you would if there was just one, for example, with **omma**, say '**om**', then, keeping your mouth closed and still making the humming sound of the **m**, make a little pause before you say '**ma**'. Just remember to try and make the consonant sound a little longer than you would if there was only one of them.

Top ten tips

1   Always remove your shoes when entering
    someone's home.

2   While eating, do not leave your chopsticks
    sticking in your rice bowl. While you are not
    using them, leave them on the table.

3   The number '4' is associated with death (as it is
    pronounced the same), so sometimes, there is
    no 4th floor in buildings.

4   When drinking with others, offer to pour their
    drinks. They will then offer to pour your drink.
    If they offer to pour your drink first, you should
    offer to pour theirs next.

5   Remember to address Koreans using the
    appropriate professional titles until specifically
    invited by your host or colleagues to use their
    given names.

6   Koreans place the family name first, and the
    given personal name second.

13

7   If at all possible, Koreans avoid calling a person
     directly by their name. Instead they use the
     title, position, trade or profession.

8   Tipping is not a traditional Korean custom, the
     service charge is generally included in the bill.

9   Always wait for the oldest person present to
     begin eating and do not leave the table until the
     oldest person has finished.

10   Use both hands when giving something to
     a Korean (especially elderly Koreans).

Talking to people

Hello/goodbye, yes/no

Hello	안녕하세요? annyong haseyo?
Goodbye	안녕히 가세요 / 안녕히 계세요 annyong(h)i kaseyo / annyong(h)i kayseyo
See you later	또 만나요 tto mannayo
See you tomorrow	내일 또 만나요 naeil tto mannayo
How are you?	안녕하세요? annyong haseyo?
Fine, thanks. And you?	네, 안녕하세요? ne, annyong haseyo?
Please	부탁합니다 pootak hamnida
Thank you	감사합니다 / 고맙습니다 kamsa-hamnida / komap-sumnida
You're welcome	천만에요 chonmaneyo

15

Excuse me!	실례합니다! sille-hamnida!
Sorry!	미안합니다! mian-hamnida!
Yes	네 ne
No	아니오 anio
Um...	음... um...
Yes, please	네, 부탁합니다 ne, pootak-hamnida
No, thanks	아니오, 괜찮아요 anio, kwenchanayo
Sir...	...씨 ...ssi
Mr...	...씨, ...선생님 ...-ssi ; ...-sonseng-nim
Mrs...	...씨, ...부인 ...-ssi ; ...-puin
Ms...	...씨 ...-ssi
I don't understand	모르겠어요 morugessoyo
I don't speak Korean	한국말 못해요 hangoongmal mot-haeyo

16

Key phrases

....

There is no gender, article nor singular/plural form
in Korean. Different counters are used together
with numbers (please see the number section for
more detail).

museum	박물관
	pangmoolkwan
the station	역
	yok
the shops	가게 / 상점
	kage/sangjom
the houses	집
	chip
a/one	하나
	hana
a ticket	표 한장
	pyo han chang
one stamp	우표 한장
	oopyo han chang
a room	방 하나
	pang hana
one bottle	한 병
	han pyong

some (countable/ uncountable)	조금 chogum
some wine	와인 조금 wain chogum
some fruit	과일 조금 kwail chogum
some biscuits	과자 조금 kwaja chogum
Do you have...?	... 있어요? ...issoyo?
Do you have a timetable?	시간표 있어요? shiganpyo issoyo?
Do you have a room?	방 있어요? pang issoyo?
Do you have milk?	우유 있어요? ooyu issoyo?
I/We'd like...	... (名詞) 주세요 ...chuseyo
I/We'd like an ice-cream	아이스크림 주세요 aisukurim chuseyo
We'd like to go home	집에 가고 싶어요 chip ey kago sipoyo
Another/ Some more...	조금 더 chogum to

18

Some more bread	빵 조금 더
	bang chogum to
Some more drinks	음료수 조금 더
	umnyosoo chogum to
Another coffee	커피 조금 더
	k'o-p'i chogum to
Another beer	맥주 조금 더
	maekchoo chogum to
Some more water	물 조금 더
	mool chogum to
How much is it?	이거 얼마예요?
	igo olmayeyo?
How much does it take?	얼마나 걸려요?
	olmana kollyoyo?
large	큰
	k'un
small	작은
	chagun
with	하고
	hago
without	없이 / 빼고
	opsi/ppaego
Where is/are...?	...어디예요?
	...odiyeyo?

Where is/are the nearest...?	제일 가까운 ... 어디예요?
	cheil kakkaun ... odiyeyo?
How do I get...?	...어떻게 가요?
	...ottok'e kayo?
to the museum	박물관에
	pangmoolkwane
to the station	역에
	yoge
to Busan	부산에
	poosane
There is/are...	... 있어요
	...issoyo
There isn't/ aren't any...	... 없어요
	...opsoyo
When?	언제?
	onje?
At what time...?	몇 시에?
	myo ssie?
today	오늘
	onul
tomorrow	내일
	naeil
Can I...?	...가능해요?
	...kanung haeyo?
smoke	흡연
	hupyon

20

taste it	시식
	shishik
How does this work?	이거 어떻게 사용해요?
	igo ottok'e sayong-haeyo?
What does this mean?	이거 무슨 뜻이에요?
	igo musun ttushi-yeyo?

Signs and notices

영업 중	open
휴업	closed
여자	ladies
남자	gentlemen
셀프 서비스	self-service
미세요	push
당기세요	pull
계산대	cash desk
음료수	drinking water
화장실	toilets
사용 중	engaged
응급치료	first aid
응급실	emergencies
일단중지	stop

고장	out of order
세일	sales
일층	basement
이층	ground floor
입구	entrance
매표소	ticket office
경찰서	police station
분실물 보관소	lost property
출발	departures
도착	arrivals
금지	prohibited
수화물 보관소	left luggage
사유, 개인	private
온수	hot (water)
냉수	cold (water)
위험	danger
금연	no smoking
만지지 마시오	do not touch
비상구	exit
탈의실	changing room
조심	caution
안내	information
안내소	enquiries

Work

. . . .

What do you do?	직업이 뭐예요? chigobi mo-yeyo?
Where's your company?	회사가 어디예요? hwesa-ga odi-yeyo?
I'm...	저는... cho-nun...
a doctor	의사예요 uisa-yeyo
a company worker	회사원이예요 hwesawon-iyeyo
a housewife	가정주부예요 kajong-chubu-yeyo
I work from home	저는 집에서 근무해요 cho-nun chibeso kunmu-haeyo
I'm self-employed	저는 자영업자예요 cho-nun chayong-opcha-yeyo

Weather

weather forecast	일기예보 ilgi-yebo
fine	좋아요 chohayo
bad	나빠요 nappayo
cloudy	흐려요 huryoyo
changeable weather	변덕스러운 날씨 pyondok-suro-un nalssi
It's sunny	날씨가 좋아요 nalssi-ga choayo
It's muggy	무더운 muto-un
It's raining	비가 와요 pi-ga wayo
It's snowing	눈이 와요 nuni wayo
It's windy	바람이 불어요 param-i puroyo
What a lovely day!	날씨가 아주 좋아요! nalssi-ga aju choayo!

English	Korean	Romanization
What awful weather!	날씨가 아주 나빠요	nalssi-ga aju nappayo!
What will the weather be like tomorrow?	내일 날씨가 어때요?	naeil nalssi-ga ottaeyo?
Do you think it's going to rain?	비가 올까요?	pi-ga olkkayo?
It's very hot today	오늘 날씨가 아주 더워요	onul nalssi-ga aju towoyo
It's very cold today	오늘 날씨가 아주 추워요	onul nalssi-ga aju chuwoyo
Do you think there will be a storm?	바람이 많이 불까요?	parami man(h)i bulkkayo
Do you think it will snow?	눈이 올까요?	nuni olkkayo?
Will it be foggy?	안개가 낄까요?	angae-ga kkil-kkayo?
What is the temperature?	기온이 얼마예요?	kioni olma-yeyo?

Weather

Getting around

Asking the way

반대	pandae	opposite
...옆에	...yo-p'ae	next to...
...가까이	...kakkai	near to...
신호등	shinho-dung	traffic lights
사거리	sagori	crossroads
골목	kol-mok	corner (of road)

FACE TO FACE

A 실례지만, 역이 어디에요?

sille-jiman, yogi odi-yeyo?

Excuse me, how do I get to the station?

B 곧장 가서, 첫번째 골목에서 왼쪽으로 도세요

kocchang kaso, chopponchae kolmogeso wenchok uro toseyo

Keep straight on, turn left at the first corner

A 멀어요?
moroyo?
Is it far?

B 아니오, 오분쯤 가요
anio, obun cchum kayo
No, about five minutes

A 감사합니다!
kamsahamnida!
Thank you!

B 천만에요
chonmaneyo
You're welcome

We're lost	길을 잃었어요
	kirul irossoyo
We're looking for...	...찾고 있어요
	...ch'ak-ko issoyo
Is this the right way to...?	...에 가는데, 이 길이 맞아요?
	...e kanunte, igiri majayo?
Can I/we walk there?	거기까지 걸어갈 수 있어요?
	kogi-kkaji koro-galsu issoyo?

How do I/we get onto the motorway?	어떻게 하면 고속도로에 갈 수 있어요? ottok'e hamyon kosok-toro-e kal-su issoyo?
How do I/we get to the museum?	어떻게 하면 박물관에 갈 수 있어요? ottok'e hamyon pangmoolkwan-e kal-su issoyo?
How do I/we get to to the shops?	어떻게 하면 가게에 갈 수 있어요? ottok'e hamyon kage-e kal-su issoyo?
Can you show me on the map?	지도에서 가르쳐 주시겠어요? chido-eso karuchyo chusigessoyo?

YOU MAY HEAR...	
앞에 ap'e	in front
뒤에 twi-e	behind
한번 더 물어보세요 hanpon to muro-poseyo	then ask again

28

Bus and coach

• •

Places like Seoul have a tourist bus and an English-language bus route map which can be obtained from a bus station. To use the local buses, you normally get on at the front door and pay into the money box as you enter. A display board at the front of the bus shows its destination. You will need to know your destination in Korean characters. Long/middle distance coach tickets, including airport limousines, are usually sold at coach station counters.

FACE TO FACE

A 실례지만 어느 버스가 시내에 가요?
   sille-jiman onu posu-ga sine-e kayo?
   Excuse me, which bus goes to the centre?

B 53번이요
   oshp-sam-pon iyo
   Number 53

A 버스 정류장은 어디예요?
   bosu chong-nyu-jang-un odi-yeyo?
   Where is the bus stop?

B 저기 오른쪽이에요
   chogi oruncchog-iyeyo
   There, on the right

B 어디서 버스표를 팔아요?

odiso p'yo-rul p'arayo?

Where can I buy the tickets?

A 저 가게에서 팔아요

cho kage-eso p'arayo

At the newsstand

Is there a bus to...?	... (에) 가는 버스가 있어요? ...(e) kanun posu-ga issoyo?
Is there tube to...?	... (에) 가는 지하철이 있어요? ...(e) kanun chihachol-i issoyo?
Where do I catch the bus to...?	어디서 ... (에) 가는 버스를 타요? odiso ... (e) kanun posu-rul t'ayo?
We would like to go to...	... (에) 가고 싶은데요 ...(e) kago sip'undeyo
Where do I catch the tram to...?	어디서 ... (에) 가는 지하철을 타요? odiso ... (e) kanun chihachol-ul t'ayo?
How much is it to go...?	... 까지 얼마예요? ...kkaji olma-yeyo?
to the centre	시내에 shine-e

30

to the beach	해변에
	haebyon-e
How often are the buses to...?	...(에) 가는 버스가 얼마나 자주 있어요?
	...(e) kanun posu-ga olmana chaju issoyo?
When is the first bus to...?	...(에) 가는 첫차가 언제 있어요?
	...(e) kanun ch'och'a -ga onje issoyo?
When is the last bus to...?	...(에) 가는 막차가 언제 있어요?
	...(e) kanun makch'a-ga onje issoyo?
Please tell me where to get off	어디서 내리는지 가르쳐 주세요
	odiso naeri-nunji karuch'yo chuseyo
Please tell me when we are at...	...(에) 도착하면 가르쳐 주세요
	...(e) toch'ak-hamyon karuch'yo chuseyo
Please let me off	미안합니다. 내려주세요
	mianhamnida. naeryo-juseyo
I got on at...	...에서 탔어요
	...eso t'assoyo

> **Luggage** (p 98)

| Sorry, I forgot to take a ticket (on entering bus) | 미안합니다. 표를 사지 않았어요
mianhamnida. p'yo-rul saji anassoyo |

YOU MAY HEAR...

| 여기 내리세요
yogi naeriseyo | This is your stop |
| 지하철이 빨라요
chihachor-i ppallayo | Take the metro, it's quicker |

Metro

The Korean metro and train services are clean, safe and run on time. You can either purchase a prepaid card or an ordinary ticket from the ticketing machine or ticketing office. In Seoul, the rush hour (between 7 and 9 am and 5 and 8 pm) crush can be really bad. The first thing you must do is obtain a metro map which indicates all the lines and stops.

입구	ip-kku	entrance
출구	ch'ul-ku	way out

Can I get a seat reservation please?	좌석 예약 부탁합니다 chwasok yeyak pootak'amnida	
Where can I get a ticket?	표는 어디서 사요? p'yo-nun odiso sayo?	
Where is the nearest metro station?	제일 가까운 지하철 역이 어디예요? cheil kakkaun chihachol yogi odi-yeyo?	
How does the ticket machine work?	자동판매 기는 어떻게 사용합니까? chadong p'anmaegi-nun ottok'e sayong-hamnikka?	
I'm going to...	...(에) 갑니다 ...(e) kamnida	
Do you have a map of the metro?	지하철 지도 있어요? chihachol chido issoyo?	
How do I get to...?	...에 어떻게 가요? ...e ottok'e kayo?	
Do I have to change?	갈아타야 돼요? karat'aya tweyo?	
Does this go to...?	이거 ... (에) 가요? igo ... (e) kayo?	

> **Luggage** (p 98)

Which line is it for...?	...행은 몇호선이예요?
	...haeng-un myot'oson iyeyo?
What is the next stop?	다음 역은 어디에요?
	taum yogun odi-yeyo?
Excuse me!	미안합니다!
	mianhamnida!
Please let me out	내려요
	naeryoyo

Train

무궁화호	intercity (stops at
mugoonghwa-ho	intercity stations)
새마을호 saemaul-ho	intercity (stops at main
	intercity stations)
KTX k'ei-t'i-eksu	high-speed intercity
	train
승강장 seunggangjang	platform
창구 ch'ang-gu	ticket office
시간표 shiganp'yo	timetable
연착 yonch'ak	delay (appears on train
	noticeboards)
수하물 soohamool	left luggage

FACE TO FACE

A ...행 다음 기차는 몇 시예요?
...haeng taum kich'a-nun myossi-yeyo?
When is the next train to...?

B 10시 25분이예요
yol-si isip-o-pun iyeyo
At 10.25

A 표 한 장 주세요
p'yo han-jang chuseyo
I'd like a ticket, please

B 편도예요, 왕복이예요?
p'yond-yeyo, wangbok-iyeyo?
Single or return?

Where is the station?	역은 어디예요? yogun odi-yeyo?
to...	...행 ...haeng
a single	편도 한 장 p'yondo han-jang
two returns	왕복 두 장 wang-bok tu-jang
reserved seat	지정석 chijong-sok

non-reserved seat	자유석
	chayu-sok
first class	일등석
	il-ttung-sok
standard class	보통
	pot'ong
smoking	흡연석
	hubyon-sok
non smoking	금연석
	kumyon-sok
I want to book a seat on Saemaul-ho train to Busan	부산까지 새마을호 좌석 하나를 예약하고 싶은데요
	poosan-kkaji saemaul-ho chwasok hanarul yeyak'ago sip'undeyo
Do I have to change?	갈아타야 되나요?
	kara t'aya twenayo?
How long is there for the connection?	갈아타는 시간은 어느 정도 있어요?
	kara t'anun shigan-un onu chongdo issoyo?
Is this the train for...?	이게 ... 행 기차예요?
	ige ... haeng kich'a-yeyo?
Why is the train delayed?	기차가 왜 지연되나요?
	kich'a-ga we chiyon-twenayo?

36

When will it leave?	언제 출발해요?
	onje ch'ulbal-haeyo?
Does it stop at...?	...에 정차합니까?
	...e chongch'a-hamnikka?
When does it arrive in...?	...에 언제 도착합니까?
	...e onje toch'ak'amnikka?
Please tell me when we get to...	...에 도착하면 가르쳐 주세요
	...e toch'ak'amyon karuch'yo chuseyo
Is there a restaurant car?	식당차가 있어요?
	shiktang-ch'a-ga issoyo?
Is this seat free?	이 자리 비어 있어요?
	i chari pio issoyo?
Excuse me! (to get past)	실례합니다!
	sillehamnida!

Taxi

. . . .

Korean taxis are safe, clean and operate on meters.
The basic fee is based on the vehicle size and type:
small grey or slightly larger black. Taxi fares are
comparatively cheap and there is no need to tip.
There are taxi stands at stations and major hotels

> **Luggage** (p 98)

but taxis can also be hailed from the roadside. You can identify whether a taxi is available by the sign 빈차 (pronounced 'pin ch'a') displayed in the front windscreen. A receipt can be requested if necessary.

I want a taxi	택시 타고 싶어요
	t'aekssi t'ago sip'oyo
Where can I get a taxi?	택시 타는 곳은 어디예요?
	t'aekssi t'anun kosun odi-yeyo?
Please order me a taxi...	...택시를 불러주세요
	...t'aekssi-rul pullo chuseyo
now	지금
	chigum
for... (time)	...(시) 에
	...(shi) e
How much will it cost to go to...?	...까지 얼마예요?
	...kkaji olma-yeyo?
How long will it take?	얼마나 걸려요?
	olmana kollyoyo?
vacant (car)	빈차
	pin ch'a
To the station please	역까지 부탁합니다
	yok-kkaji poot'ak'amnida
To the airport please	공항까지 부탁합니다
	konghang-kkaji poot'ak'amnida

38

To this address please	이 주소까지 부탁합니다 i chuso-kkaji poot'ak'amnida
How much is it?	얼마예요? olma-yeyo?
Can I have a receipt please?	영수증 부탁합니다 yongsu-jung poot'ak'amnida
Keep the change	잔돈은 됐어요 chan-don-un twessoyo
Sorry, I don't have any change	미안합니다. 잔돈이 없어요 mianhamnida. chan-don-i opssoyo
I'm in a hurry	좀 급합니다 chom kup'amnida
Can you go a little faster?	더 빨리 가 주시겠어요? to ppalli ka chusigessoyo?
I have to catch...	...를 타야 돼요 ...rul t'aya tweyo
a train	기차 kich'a
a plane	비행기 pihaeng-gi

> **Luggage** (p 98)

Boat and ferry

• •

Do you have a timetable?	시간표 있어요? shigan-p'yo issoyo?
Is there a car ferry to...?	...행 카페리 있어요? ...haeng k'a-p'eri issoyo?
How much is a ... ticket?	표는 얼마예요? ...p'yo-nun olma-yeyo?
single	편도 p'yondo
return	왕복 wangbok
How much is it for a car and ... people?	자동차하고 ... 사람 얼마예요? chadong-ch'a hago ... saram olma-yeyo?
one (person)	한 (사람) han (saram)
two (people)	두 (사람) too (saram)
three (people)	세 (사람) se (saram)
Where does the boat leave from?	배가 어디서 출발해요? pae-ga odiso ch'ulpal-haeyo?

Are there any boat trips?	유람선 있어요? yooram-son issoyo?
When is the next boat?	다음 배는 언제예요? taum pae-nun onje-yeyo?
How long does the trip take?	시간은 얼마나 걸려요? shigan-un olmana kollyoyo?

YOU MAY HEAR...

이게 마지막 배예요 ige majimak pae-yeyo	This is the last boat
오늘은 끝났어요 onur-un kkunnassoyo	There is no service today
무슨 자동차예요? musun chadongch'a-yeyo?	What type of car do you have?

Air travel

At the airport, most signs are written in both Korean
and English. All the airport staff understand and
speak some English. You can find airport details by
visiting **www.airport.or.kr** or
gimpo.airport.co.kr, for example.

도착	toch'ak	arrivals
출발	ch'ulpal	departures
국제	kook-che	international
국내	koong-nae	domestic
탑승구	t'apsung-gu	boarding gate

How do I/we get to the airport?	공항까지는 어떻게 가요?	konghang-kkaji-nun ottok'e kayo?
How do I/we get to town?	시내까지는 어떻게 가요?	shine-kkaji-nun ottok'e kayo?
How do I/we get to the ... hotel?	호텔까지는 어떻게 가요?	hotel-kkaji-nun ottok'e kayo?
Is there a bus to the airport?	공항 가는 버스 있어요?	konghang kanun posu issoyo?
How much is it by taxi to...?	...까지 택시로 얼마예요?	...kkaji t'aekssi-ro olma-yeyo?

Where is the check-in desk for...?	...체크인 데스크는 어디예요? ...ch'e-k'u-in desuk'u-nun odi-yeyo?
Which luggage belt is the luggage on for the flight from...?	...에서 도착한 수하물은 어디 있어요? ...eso toch'ak'an soohamoor-un odi issoyo?
Where can I change some money?	외국돈 교환은 어디서 합니까? weguk-ton kyohwan-un odiso hamnikka?

YOU MAY HEAR...

...번 게이트에서 출발합니다 ...pon keit'u-eso ch'ulpal-hamnida	Boarding will take place at gate number...
...번 게이트까지 빨리 가주시기 바랍니다 ...pon keit'u-kkaji ppalli ka chusigi paramnida	Go immediately to gate number...

43

Customs control

· ·

UK, US ,Canadian and Australian visitors to Korea
do not require a visa for short business trips and
holidays. During your stay, you are not allowed to
work. Korean law requires you to carry proof of
identity at all times, so make sure that you always
carry your passport.

내국인 nae-goo-gin	Koreans returning to the country
외국인 we-goo-gin	Foreigners entering the country
관세 kwanse	customs

Do I have to pay duty on this?	여기 세금이 포함돼 있어요? yogi segumi p'oham twe issoyo?
It's for my own personal use	제가 사용할 거예요 che-ga sayonghal go-yeyo
It's a present	선물이에요 sonmoor-i yeyo
I have nothing to declare	신고할 게 없어요 shingohal ge opssoyo

 > **Luggage** (p 98)

We are on our way to... (if in transit through a country)	...로 가는 도중이예요 ...ro kanun tojung-i yyeyo
The child/children is/are also on this passport	아이도 이 여권에 있어요 ai-do i yokwon-e issoyo
My passport	제 여권 che yokwon
My visa	제 비자 che picha
I came here on holiday	휴가 왔어요 hyuga wassoyo
I came here on business	출장 왔어요 chuljang wassoyo

Driving

Car hire

Driving

| 운전면허증
oonjon myonho-cchung | driving licence |
| 종합보험
chonghap pohom | fully comprehensive
insurance |

I want to hire a car for 3 days	3일 간 렌트카하고 싶어요 samil gan ren-t'u-k'a hago sip'oyo

I want to hire
  a car with
  automatic gears
	오토로 렌트카하고 싶어요
	ot'o-ro ren-t'u-k'a hago sip'oyo

What are your rates...?	...요금이 얼마예요? ...yogumi olma-yeyo?
per day	하루에 haru-e
per week	일주일에 ilcchuire

How much is the deposit?	보증금은 얼마예요?
	pojunggum-un olma-yeyo?
Do you take credit cards?	신용카드 받아요?
	sinyong k'adu padayo?
Is there a mileage (kilometre) charge?	주행거리 할증료도 있어요?
	chuhaeng-gori halchung-nyo-do issoyo?
How much is it?	얼마예요?
	olma-yeyo?
Does the price include fully comprehensive insurance?	종합보험금도 포함돼 있어요?
	chonghap pohomgum-do p'oham twe issoyo?
Must I return the car here?	차는 여기에 다시 반환해야 돼요?
	ch'a-nun yogi-e tashi panhwan haeya tweyo?
By what time?	몇 시까지요?
	mossi-kkaji-yo?
I'd like to leave it in...	저는 ... 에 차를 반환하고 싶어요
	cho-nun ... e ch'a-rul panhwan hago sip'oyo

Car hire

47

차는 기름을 만땅 채워서 돌려 주세요 ch'a-nun kirum-ul manttang ch'ewoso tollyo chuseyo	Please return the car with a full tank

Driving and petrol

In Korea, the majority of petrol stations are manned by attendants who not only fill up the tank for you but also wipe the windows and check the water.

Can I/we park here?	여기 주차해도 돼요? yogi chuch'a haedo tweyo?
How long for?	얼마동안요? olma-dong-an-yo?
Which junction is it for...?	...로 가려면 어느 길로 가야 돼요? ...ro karyomyon onu kil-lo kaya tweyo?
Do I/we need snow chains?	스노우 체인이 필요해요? suno-u ch'e-in-i p'iryo haeyo?

Driving

Fill it up, please	만땅/가득 부탁합니다
	manttang/kaduk poot'ak'amnida
Please check the oil	오일 체크 부탁합니다
	o-il ch'e-k'u poot'ak'amnida
Please check the water	냉각수 체크 부탁합니다
	naeng-gakssoo ch'e-k'u poot'ak'amnida
30,000 won worth of unleaded petrol	삼만원 어치 무연 부탁합니다 samman-won och'i muyon poot'ak'amnida
Where is...?	...어디에 있어요?
	...odie issoyo?
the air line	에어 가
	e-o-ga
the water	물이、냉각수가
	moor-i, naeng-gak-soo-ga
Can I pay by credit card?	신용 카드 받아요?
	sinyong k'a-du padayo?

오일이 필요합니다 oiri p'iro hamnida	You need some oil
냉각수가 필요합니다 naeng-gak-soo-ga p'iro hamnida	You need some water
전부 좋아요 chonboo cho-ayo	Everything is OK

Breakdown

• •

If you break down, the emergency phone number
for the Korean equivalent of the AA (KAF – Korean
Automobile Federation) is **02 565 7001**

Can you help me?	도와 주세요? towa chuseyo?	
My car has broken down	자동차가 고장났어요 chadong-ch'a-ga kojang nassoyo	
I've run out of petrol	기름이 없어요 kirum-i opssoyo	

Can you tow me to the nearest garage?	제일 가까운 주유소까지 데려다 주세요 cheil kakkaun chuyuso-kkaji teryoda chuseyo
Do you have parts for a (make of car)...?	...부품 있어요? ...pup'um issoyo?
There's something wrong with the...	...에 이상이 있어요 ...e isang-i issoyo
Can you replace...?	...바꿔 주세요 ...pakkwo chuseyo

Car parts

| The ... isn't/aren't working properly | ...상태가 안 좋아요
...sangt'ae-ga an cho-ayo |

accelerator	가속 페달	kasok pedal
alternator	교류기	kyoryuki
battery	배터리	beteri
bonnet	본닛	bonnit
brakes	브레이크	bureiku

choke	초크	choku
clutch	클러치	kuruchi
engine	엔진	enjin
exhaust	배기장치	begijangchi
fuse	퓨즈	pyuzu
gears	기어	gia
handbrake	핸드브레이크	hendu bureiku
headlights	헤드라이트	hedu raitu
ignition	점화장치	jomhwajangchi
indicator	인디케이터	indikeito
points	포인트	pointu
radiator	라디에이터	radieito
reverse gear	백 기어	bek gia
seat belt	안전벨트	anjon beltu
spark plug	점화 플러그	jomhwa pulugu
steering	스티링	sutiring
steering wheel	핸들	hendl
tyre	타이어	taio
wheel	바퀴	bakwi
windscreen	앞 유리	amnyuri
windscreen washer	앞 유리 워셔	amnyuri wosho
windscreen wiper	앞 유리 와이퍼	amnyuri wa-i-p'o

Staying somewhere

Hotel (booking)

Korea offers a wide choice of places to stay, from western style hotels to traditional Korean inns. Some examples of these are:

장 chang, 여관 yogwan, 여인숙 yoinsuk, 민박 minbak. Minbak is often translated as B&B, but it is not correct. They are simply guest rooms in private houses – the cheapest option.

싱글 룸	sing-gul room	single room
더블 룸	tobul room	double room
침대방	ch'imdae-pang	western style room
온돌	ondol	Korean style room
어른/대인	orun/tae-in	adults
어린이	orin-i	children

FACE TO FACE

A 더블룸 예약 부탁합니다
tobul room yeyak poot'ak'amnida
I'd like to book a double room

B 몇일입니까?
myoch'ir-imnikka?
For how many nights?

A 일박입니다
il-pak-imnida
For one night

How much is it per night?	일박에 얼마예요? il-pak-e olma-yeyo?
How much is it per week?	일주일에 얼마예요? il-cchu-ir-e olma-yeyo?
Do you have a room for tonight?	오늘밤 빈방 있어요? onul pam pin pang issoyo?
with bath	욕실 있는 yok-ssil innun
with shower	샤워 있는 syawo innun
with a double bed	더블 침대 있는 tobul ch'imdae innun

54

twin-bedded with an extra bed for a child	트윈 침대하고 어린이용 침대 t'uwin ch'imdae hago orin-i-yong ch'imdae
Is breakfast included?	아침 식사도 포함돼 있어요? ach'im shiksa-do p'oham twe issoyo?
Have you anything cheaper?	더 싼 거 없어요? to ssan-go opssoyo?
I'd like to see the room	방을 보고 싶어요 pang-ul pogo sip'oyo

YOU MAY HEAR...

빈 방 없어요 pin pang opsoyo	We're full
성함/이름이 어떻게 되세요? songham/irum-i ottok'e tweseyo?	Your name, please
...확인 부탁합니다 ...hwa-gin poot'ak'amnida	Please confirm...
이메일로 i-meil-lo	by e-mail
팩스로 p'aeksu-ro	by fax

Hotel desk

••

The Korean National Tourist Organization and
Tourist Information Centre can help with finding
accommodation.

I booked a room in the name of...	...이름으로 방을 예약했어요 ...irum-uro pang-ul yeyak'aessoyo
Where can I park the car?	주차장이 어디예요? chu-ch'a-jang-i odi-yeyo?
What time is...?	...은 몇시예요? ...un myossi-yeyo?
dinner	석식 sok-shik
breakfast	조식 choshik
The key, please	열쇠 부탁합니다 yol-swe poot'ak'amnida
Room number...	방 번호는... pang ponho-nun...
Are there any messages for me?	저한테 메세지 있어요? cho-hant'e messeji issoyo?
Can I send a fax?	팩스 가능해요? p'aek-su kanung-haeyo?

56

I'm leaving tomorrow	내일 떠나요 naeil ttonayo
Please prepare the bill	계산서 부탁합니다 kesanso poot'ak'amnida

Camping

....

쓰레기	ssu-re-gi	rubbish
음료수	um-nyo-soo	drinking water
콘센트	k'on-sen-t'u	electric point

Is there a restaurant on the campsite?	캠핑장에 식당 있어요? k'em-p'ing-jang-e shik-tang issoyo?
Is there a self-service café on the campsite?	캠핑장에 셀프서비스 식당 있어요? k'em-p'ing-jang-e selp'u sobisu shik-tang issoyo?
Do you have any vacancies?	빈 자리 있어요? pin chari issoyo?
How much is it per night?	일박에 얼마예요? il-pak-e olma-yeyo?

How much is it per night per tent?	텐트당 일박에 얼마예요?	t'en-t'u-dang il-pak-e olma-yeyo?
How much is it per night per caravan?	캬라반당 일박에 얼마예요?	k'ya-raban-dang il-pak-e olma-yeyo?
How much is it per night per person?	일인당 일박에 얼마예요?	irin-dang il-pak-e olma-yeyo?
Does the price include...?	...요금은 포함돼 있어요?	...yogum-un p'oham twe issoyo?
showers	샤워	syawo
hot water	온수	onsoo
electricity	전기	chon-gi
We'd like to stay for ... nights	...동안 있을 거예요	...tong-an issul go-yeyo

58

Self-catering

● ●

Who do we contact if there are problems?	문제가 있으면 누구한테 물어볼까요? munje-ga issumyon nugu-hant'e murobol-kkayo?
How does the heating work?	히터는 어떻게 사용하나요? hit'o-nun ottok'e sayong-hanayo?
Is there always hot water?	온수는 항상 나와요? onsoo-nun hangsang nawayo?
Where is the nearest supermarket?	제일 가까운 수퍼마켓은 어디예요? cheil kakkaun sup'o-mak'e-sun odi-yeyo?
Where do we leave the rubbish?	쓰레기는 어디에 버려요? ssuregi-nun odi-e poryoyo?

> **Sightseeing and tourist office** (p 74)

Shopping

Shopping phrases

Opening hours are approximately 9.30 am to
6.30 pm with slightly longer opening hours at the
weekends, in summer and at the end of the year.
Some supermarkets are open 24 hours a day.

Shopping

FACE TO FACE

A 뭘 찾으세요?
  mwol ch'ajuseyo?
  What would you like?

B ...있어요?
  ...issoyo?
  Do you have...?

A 네, 여기 있어요. 다른 건요?
  ne, yogi issoyo. tarun gon-yo?
  Certainly, here you are. Anything else?

60

Where is...?	...은 어디 있어요?
	...un odi issoyo?
I'm just looking	그냥 구경하고 있어요
	kunyang ku-gyong hago issoyo
I'm looking for	...(의) 선물을 찾고 있어요
a present for...	...(e) sonmur-ul ch'a-kko issoyo
my mother	어머니
	omoni
a child	아이들
	aidul
Where can I buy...?	...은 어디서 팔아요?
	...un odiso p'arayo?
shoes	구두
	kudu
gifts	선물
	sonmool
Do you have	좀 ... 거 있어요?
anything...?	chom ... go issoyo?
larger	큰
	k'un
smaller	작은
	chagun
It's too expensive	너무 비싸요
for me	nomu pissayo
Can you give me	디스카운트 해주세요
a discount?	tisu-k'aun-t'u hae chuseyo

Shops

....

세일 sse-il	**sale**
할인 harin	**discount**
(금일) 휴업 (kumil) hyu-op	**closed** (for today)

baker's	제과점 / 빵집	che-kwa-jom/ ppangchip
bookshop	서점	suh-jom
butcher's	정육점	chong-yuk-jom
cake shop	제과점	che-kwa-jom
clothes	양복 / 양장점	yang-bok (men's)/ yangjang-jom (women's)
fruit shop	과일 가게	kwail kage
gifts	선물 가게	sonmool kage
grocer's	식료품점	shingnyo-p'um-jom
hairdresser's	이발소 / 미장원	ipalso (men's)/ mijang-won (women's)
newsagent's	신문 가게	shimmun kage
optician's	안경점	an-gyong-jom

62

cosmetic shop	화장품 가게	hwajang-p'um kage
pharmacy	약국	yakkuk
photographic shop	사진관	sajin-kwan
shoe shop	제화점 / 신발가게	che-hwa-jom/ shinbal kage
sports shop	스포츠샵	sup'o-ch'u-syap
supermarket	수퍼마켓	sup'o mak'et
tobacconist's	담배 가게	tambae kage
toys	장난감 가게	chang-nan-gam kage

Food (general)

biscuits	과자	kwaja
black pepper	후추	huchu
bread	빵	ppang
bread (for toast)	식빵	shik ppang
butter	버터	bot'o
cheese	치즈	ch'i-ju
chicken	닭, 치킨	tak, chikin (fast-food)
coffee (instant)	커피	k'o-p'i

cream	크림	k'u-rim
crisps	감자튀김, 후렌치 후라이	kamja t'wi-gim, hurenchi hurai (fast-food)
eggs	달걀	tal-gyal
fish	생선	saeng-son
ham	햄	haem
herbal tea	허브차	hobucha
hot sauce	고추장	gochujang
jam	잼	cham
juice, orange	쥬스, 오렌지	choosu, orenji
margarine	마가린	magarin
marmalade	마마레이드	mama-re-i-du
milk	우유	oo-yoo
mustard	겨자	gyeoja
oil	식용유	shi-gyong-nyu
pepper	후추	hoo-ch'oo
salt	소금	sogum
soya sauce	간장	ganjang
soya bean paste	된장	doenjang
sugar	설탕	solt'ang
Korean tea	녹차	nok-ch'a
English tea	홍차	hong-ch'a
vinegar	식초	shik-ch'o
yoghurt	요구르트	yo-gu-ru-t'u

> **Measurements and quantities** (p 118)

Food (fruit and veg)

Fruit

apples	사과	sakwa
apricots	살구	salkoo
bananas	바나나	banana
cherries	앵두	aeng-doo
grapefruit	자몽	cha-mong
grapes	포도	p'o-do
lemon	레몬	re-mon
melon	멜론 / 참외	meron/ch'am-we
oranges	오렌지	orenji
peaches	복숭아	pok-sung-a
pears	배	pae
plums	자두	cha-doo
raspberries	산딸기	san-ttalgi
strawberries	딸기	ttalgi
watermelon	수박	soobak

Vegetables

asparagus	아스파라가스	asuparagasu
aubergine	가지	kaji
carrots	당근	tang-gun
cauliflower	컬리프라워	k'ol-li-p'ul-la-wo
celery	셀러리	sel-lori
courgettes	호박	hobak
cucumber	오이	o-i
garlic	마늘	manul
leeks	파	pa
mushrooms	버섯	posot
onions	양파	yang-p'a
peas	완두콩	wanduk'ong
pepper	후추	hoo-ch'oo
potatoes	감자	kamja
salad	샐러드	sael-lo-du
spinach	시금치	shigumch'i
tomatoes	토마토	t'omat'o

Clothes

....

FACE TO FACE

A 입어봐도 돼요?
ipo pwado tweyo?
May I try this on?

B - 물론이예요, 이리 오세요
muloniyeyo, iri oseyo
Of course, please come this way

A 미디움 사이즈 있어요?
midium ssa-i-ju issoyo?
Do you have a medium size?

Where are the changing rooms?	탈의실이 어디 있어요? taruishiri odi issoyo?
Have you a size...?	...사이즈 있어요? ...ssa-i-ju issoyo?
bigger	더 큰 to k'un
smaller	더 작은 to chagun
Have you this...?	이 옷 ... 으로 있어요? i ot ... uro issoyo?

67

in my size	내 사이즈 (로)
	nae ssa-i-ju (ro)
in other colours	다른 색 (으로)
	tarun saek (uro)
That's a shame!	유감인데요
	yougam indeyo
It's too...	너무...
	nomu...
short	짧아요
	jjalbayo
long	길어요
	kiroyo
I'm just looking	그냥 구경하고 있어요
	kunyang ku-gyong hago issoyo
I'll take it	사겠어요
	sagetsoyo

YOU MAY HEAR...

무슨 사이즈?	What size?
musun ssa-i-ju?	
입어 보실래요?	Do you want to try it on?
ibo boshil-leyo?	
맞아요?	Does it fit?
majayo?	

68

이 색깔은 이 사이즈밖에 없어요 i saek-kkar-un i ssa-i-ju pakke opssoyo	In this colour we only have this size
사이즈가 뭐예요? ssa-i-ju-ga mwo-yeyo?	What size (clothes) do you take?
구두 사이즈가 뭐예요? kudu ssa-i-ju-ga mwo-yeyo?	What shoe size do you take?

Clothes (articles)

belt	혁대	hyukdae
blouse	블라우스	burausu
bra	브라자	brasa
coat	코트 / 외투	k'o-t'u/we-t'u
dress	드레스	du-re-su
hat	모자	moja
jacket	자켓	cha-k'et
jumper	점퍼	chom-p'o
knickers	속옷	sogot
nightdress	잠옷	chamot
pyjamas	잠옷	chamot
sandals	샌달	sendal

Clothes (articles)

> **Paying** (p 96) > **Numbers** (p 120)

scarf	스카프	sukapu
shirt	셔츠	syo-ch'u
shorts	반바지	pan paji
skirt	치마	ch'ima
slippers	슬리퍼	suripu
socks	양말	yangmal
suit	양복	yangbok
swimsuit	수영복	soo-yong-bok
tie	넥타이	nektai
tights	팬티 스타킹	penti staking
tracksuit	운동복	undongbok
trousers	바지	paji
t-shirt	티셔츠	t'i syo-ch'u
underpants	속바지	sogbaji

Maps and guides

잡지 chap-chi	magazine
주간지 chugan-ji	a weekly magazine
월간지 wolgan-ji	a monthly magazine
신문 shimmun	newspaper

Do you have a map...?	...지도 있어요?
	...chido issoyo?
of the town	시내
	shinae
of the region	이 지역
	I chiyok
Can you show me where ... is on the map?	...는 이 지도에서 어디 있어요?
	...nun I chido-eso odi issoyo?
Do you have a guidebook in English?	영어 안내서 있어요?
	yong-o annaeso issoyo?
Do you have a leaflet in English?	영어로 된 팸플릿 있어요?
	yong-o ro dwen pampulet issoyo?
Do you have any English newspapers?	영어 신문 있어요?
	yong-o shimmun issoyo?
Do you have any English books?	영어로 된 책 있어요?
	yong-o ro dwen chaek issoyo?

> **Asking the way** (p 26)
> **Sightseeing and tourist office** (p 74)

Post office

Post office opening hours vary but they are usually from 9.00 am to 5.00 pm, Monday to Friday. Some post offices in the main cities open until around 7.00 pm and at weekends.

우체국	oo-ch'e-guk	**post office**
우표	oo-p'yo	**stamps**
속달	sok-tal	**first class post**

Where is the post office?	우체국이 어디예요? oo-ch'e-gugi odi-yeyo?
When does it open?	언제 열어요? onje yoroyo?
Which is the counter...?	...카운터는 어디예요? ...k'a-un-t'o-nun odi-yeyo?
for stamps	우표 oo-p'yo
for parcels	소포 sop'o
6 stamps for postcards...	엽서용 우표 여섯 장 yopso-yong oop'yo yosot chang

for Britain	영국
	yong-guk
for America	미국
	miguk
for Australia	호주
	hoju

YOU MAY HEAR...

문방구에서 우표 팔아요	You can buy stamps
munbang-goo-eso oo-p'yo	at the stationery
parayo	shop

Photos

. . . .

A tape for this camcorder	이 캠코더의 테이프
	i k'em-k'o-do-e t'e-i-p'u
Do you have batteries for this camera?	이 카메라 건전지 있어요?
	i k'a-me'ra konjonji issoyo?

> **Money** (p 94) > **Paying** (p 96) 73

Leisure

Sightseeing and tourist office

· ·

The Korean National Tourist Organisation has a
great deal of information. Visit **www.knto.or.kr**

Where is the tourist office?	관광 안내소가 어디예요? kwangwang annaeso-ga odi-yeyo?
What can we visit in the area?	이 근처에 관광 명소가 있어요? i kunch'o-e kwangwang myongso-ga issoyo?
in two hours	두 시간 안에 tu shigan an-e
Have you any leaflets?	안내서 있어요? annaeso issoyo?
Are there any excursions?	가이드 관광이 있어요? kaidu kwangwang-i issoyo?
We'd like to go to...	...에 가고 싶은데요 ...e kago sip'undeyo

How much does it cost to get in?	입장료가 얼마예요? ipchang-nyo-ga olma-yeyo?
Are there reductions for...?	...디스카운트 있어요? ...ti-su-k'a-un-t'u issoyo?
children	아이들 aidul
students	학생 haksaeng
over 60s	육십세 이상 yuk-sip-se isang

Entertainment

What is there to do in the evenings?	밤에는 뭐가 재미있어요? pam-enun mwo-ga chaemi issoyo?
Do you have a programme of events?	재미있는 프로그램 있어요? chaemi innun p'u-ro-gu-raem-i issoyo?
Is there anything for children?	아이들을 위한 것도 있어요? aidur-ul wihan got-to issoyo?

> **Maps and guides** (p 70)

Leisure/interests

●●●●●●●●●●●●●●●●●●●●●●●●●●●●●●●●●

Where can I/ we go...?	...은 어디서 가능해요?
	...un odiso kanung-haeyo?
fishing	낚시
	nak-ssi
walking	산보
	sam-po
Are there any good beaches near here?	이 근처에 좋은 해변이 있어요?
	i kunch'o-e cho-un haebyon-i issoyo?
Is there a swimming pool?	수영장 있어요?
	soo-yong-jang issoyo?

Music

Are there any good concerts on?   좋은 음악회 있어요?
cho-un umak'we issoyo?

Where can I get tickets for the concert?   음악회 표는 어디서 팔아요?
umak'we p'yo-nun odiso p'arayo?

Where can we hear some classical music?   클래식 음악은 어디서 해요?
k'ul-lae-shik umak -un odiso haeyo?

Where can we hear some jazz?   재즈는 어디서 해요?
chaeju-nun odiso haeyo?

Cinema

영화관   yongwha-gwan   cinema

What's on at the cinema (name of cinema)...?   (...) 영화관에서 무슨 영화 해요?
(...) yonghwa-gwan-eso musun yonghwa haeyo?

What time does the film start?	영화는 몇 시에 시작해요? yonghwa-nun myo-ssi-e shijak'haeyo?
How much are the tickets?	표는 얼마예요? p'yo-nun olma-yeyo?
Tickets for two adults	...어른 두 장 ...orun tu chang

(number) 상영실 표는 매진됐어요 (number) sangyongshil pyo-nun maejin-twe-ssoyo	We have no tickets left for screen (number)

Leisure

Theatre/opera

Major hotels can get theatre and opera tickets for
you, or you can buy them at ticketing offices in
stations or travel agencies. You can also search and
buy any tickets on the internet.

S석	esu-sok	superior seat
A석	ei-sok	class A seat
B석	pi-sok	standard seat

What is on at the theatre?	이 극장에서 뭘 해요? i kukchang-eso mwol haeyo?
What prices are the tickets?	표는 얼마예요? p'yo-nun olma-yeyo?
I'd like two tickets...	...표 두 장 부탁합니다 ...p'yo tu chang poot'ak'amnida
for tonight	오늘밤 onul pam
for tomorrow night	내일밤 naeil pam
for the 3rd of August	8월 3일 p'al wol sam il

| When does the performance begin? | 연극이 언제 시작해요?
yon-gugi onje shijak'haeyo? |
| When does the performance end? | 연극이 언제 끝나요?
yon-gugi onje kkun-nayo? |

YOU MAY HEAR...

| 벌써 공연 시작해서 입장할 수 없어요
polsso kong-yon shijak'aeso ip-chang hal-soo opssoyo | You can't go in as the performance has started |
| 휴식 시간에 입장할 수 있어요
hyushik shigane ip-chang hal-soo issoyo | You may enter at the interval |

Leisure

Television

....

시리즈	siriju	series
연속극	yonsok-kuk	soap
뉴스	nyu-su	news
리모콘	rimokon	remote control
켜요	kyoyo	to switch on
꺼요	kkoyo	to switch off
프로그램	purogrem	programme

Where is the television?	테레비는 어디 있어요? t'e-re-bi-nun odi issoyo?
When is the news?	뉴스는 언제 해요? nyu-su-nun onje haeyo?
May I turn the volume up?	소리를 좀 크게 해도 돼요? sorirul chom kuge haedo dweyo?
What is on television?	테레비에서 지금 뭐 해요? t'e-re-bi-eso chigum mwo haeyo?
Do you have any English-language channels?	영어 방송도 있어요? yong-o pangsong-do issoyo?
Do you have any English videos?	영어 비디오 있어요? yong-o pi-di-o issoyo?

Sport

Where can we go...?	어디서 ... 할 수 있어요? odiso ... halsu issoyo?
swimming	수영 soo-yong
jogging	조깅 cho-ging
Do we have to be members?	회원만 가능해요? hwe-won-man kanung-haeyo?
How much is it per hour?	한 시간에 얼마예요? han shigane olma-yeyo?
Can we hire...?	...을 빌려줘요? ...ul pilyo-jwoyo?
rackets	라켓 ra-k'et
golf clubs	골프 클럽 kol-p'u k'ul-lop
We'd like to see (name team) play	...(의) 경기를 보고 싶어요 ...(e) kyong-gi-rul pogo sip'oyo
Where can I/we get tickets for the game?	이 경기의 표는 어디서 팔아요? i kyong-gi-e p'yo-nun odiso p'arayo?

이 경기의 표는
매진됐어요
i kyong-gi-e p'yo-nun
maejin-twe-ssoyo

There are no tickets
left for the game

Skiing

I want to hire skis	스키 빌리고 싶어요 su-k'i pil-ligo sip'oyo
Does the price include boots?	부츠 가격은 포함돼 있어요? poo-ch'u kagyo-gun p'oham twe issoyo?
How much is a ... pass?	...가격은 얼마예요? ...ka-gyo-gun olma-yeyo?
daily	일일권 iril-kwon
weekly	일주일권 ilchuil-kwon
What time is the last ascent lift?	마지막 리프트는 몇시예요? majimak ri-p'u-t'u-nun myossi-yeyo?

Can you adjust my bindings?

벨트를 좀 조정해
주시겠어요?

pel-t'u-rul chom
chojong-hae-jusigessoyo?

YOU MAY HEAR...	
전에 스키 타 보신 적 있어요? chon-e su-k'i t'a posin-jok issoyo?	Have you ever skied before?
어떤 스키를 원하세요? otton su-k'i-rul wonha-seyo?	What length skis do you want?
부츠/신발 사이즈가 얼마예요? poo-ch'u/shibal sa-i-ju-ga olma-yeyo?	What is your boot size?
스키 레슨을 받고 싶으세요? su-k'i le-sun-ul pak-ko sip'u-seyo?	Do you want skiing lessons?

Walking

....

English	Korean	Romanization
Are there any guided walks?	가이드 투어가 있어요?	ka-i-du t'u-o-ga issoyo?
Do you know any good walks?	산보하기 좋은 데 있어요?	sampohagi choun-de issoyo?
How many kilometres is the walk?	거리가 얼마나 돼요?	kori-ga olmana tweyo?
Is it very steep?	길이 험해요?	kir-i homhaeyo?
How long will it take?	얼마나 걸려요?	olmana kollyoyo?
Is there a map of the walk?	산책로 지도가 있어요?	sanchaeng-no chido-ga issoyo?
We'd like to go climbing	등산하고 싶어요	tungsan hago sip'oyo
Do you have a detailed map of the area?	이 지역의 자세한 지도가 있어요?	i chiyog-e chasehan chido-ga issoyo?

> **Maps and guides** (p 70)

Communications

Telephone and mobile

The international dialling code for Korea is **00 82**
plus the Korean city or area code less the first **0**,
for example, Seoul **(0)2**, Busan **(0)51**. Korean public
telephones are very good and you can make
international calls from them. You will need to use
100 won coins or buy an appropriate telephone card
from a shop or a vending machine.

전화카드 chon-hwa k'a-du	phonecard
공중전화 kong-jung chon-hwa	public phone
휴대폰 / 휴대전화 hyudae p'on / hyudae chon-hwa	mobile
전화번호부 chonhwa ponhobu	phone directory
받아요 padayo	to pick up
끊어요 kkunuyo	to hang up

FACE TO FACE

A 안녕하세요?
annyonghaseyo?
Hello?

B ...씨, 부탁합니다
...ssi, poot'ak'amnida
I'd like to speak to..., please

A 누구세요?
nuku-seyo?
Who's calling?

B 안젤라예요
anjella-yeyo
It's Angela

A 잠깐 기다리세요...
chamkkan kidariseyo...
Just a moment...

I want to make a phone call	전화 걸고 싶어요 chonhwa kolgo sip'oyo
Where can I buy a phonecard?	전화카드는 어디서 팔아요? chonhwa k'a-du-nun odiso p'arayo?
A phonecard	전화카드 chonhwa k'a-du
for ... won	...원 짜리 ...won cchari

Do you have a mobile?	휴대폰 있어요? hyudae p'on issoyo?
What is the number of your mobile?	휴대폰 번호가 뭐예요? hyudae p'on ponho-ga mwo-yeyo?
My mobile number is...	제 휴대폰 번호는 ... 이예요 che hyudae p'on ponho-nun ... i yeyo
Mr Brown, please	브라운씨 부탁합니다 pu-ra-un-ssi poot'ak'amnida
extension...	내선 ... 번 naeson ... bon
Can I speak to...?	...씨 부탁합니다 ...ssi poot'ak'amnida
I'll call back later	나중에 다시 할게요 najung-e tashi halkkeyo
I'll call back tomorrow	내일 다시 할게요 naeil tashi halkkeyo
This is Mr.../Mrs...	저는 ... 이예요 cho-nun ... i yeyo
How do I get an outside line?	외부 전화는 어떻게 사용해요? webu chonhwa-nun ottok'e sayong-haeyo?

연결해 드리겠습니다 yon-gyol hae turigessumnida	I'm trying to connect you
통화중입니다 t'ong-hwa-jung imnida	The line is engaged
다시 해 주시기 바랍니다 tashi hae chusigi paramnida	Please try later
메세지를 남기시겠습니까? me-se-ji-rul namgisi-gessumnikka?	Do you want to leave a message?
...삐소리가 난 후 메세지를 남겨 주시기 바랍니다 ...ppi sori-ga nan hu me-se-ji-rul namgyo chusigi paramnida	...leave a message after the tone
휴대 전화를 꺼 주시기 바랍니다 hyudae chonhwa-rul kko chusigi paramnida	Please turn off your mobile phone

Telephone and mobile

89

Text messaging

I will text you   메세지를 보냅니다
       me-se-ji-rul ponaemnida

Can you text me?   저한테 메세지를 보내
        주시겠습니까?
        cho-hant'e me-se-ji-rul ponae
        chusi-gessumnikka?

E-mail

To:	수신 sushin
From:	보낸 사람
	ponen saram
Subject:	제목 chemok
cc:	참조 cham-jo
bcc:	숨은 참조
	sumun cham-jo
Attachment:	파일 첨부
	p'a-il chom-bu
Send:	보내기 po-ne-gi

Do you have an e-mail?	이메일 있어요?
	i-me-il issoyo?
What is your e-mail address?	이메일 주소가 뭐예요?
	I -me-il chuso-ga mwo-yeyo?
How do you spell it?	스펠링 좀 말해 주세요
	su-p'el-ling chom malhae chuseyo
All one word	한 단어예요
	han tano-yeyo
All lower case	소문자예요
	somunja-yeyo
My e-mail address is...	이메일 주소는 ... 예요
	i-me-il chuso-nun ... yeyo
clare.smith@ bit.co.uk	clare 점 smith 골뱅이 bit 점 co 점 uk
	clare chom smith kol-paeng-i bit chom co chom uk
Can I send an e-mail?	이메일 보내도 돼요?
	i-me-il ponedo tweyo?
Did you get my e-mail?	제 이메일 받으셨어요?
	che i-me-il padu-ssyo-sso-yo?

E-mail

91

Internet

• •

Computer and Internet terminology tends to be in English.

Are there any internet cafés here?	이 근처에 인터넷 카페 있어요?
	i kunch'o-e in-t'o-net k'a-p'e issoyo?
How much is it to log on for an hour?	한 시간에 얼마예요?
	han shigan-e olma-yeyo?

Fax

• •

The international dialling code to send faxes to
Korea is **00 82** plus the Korean area code without
the first o, for example, Seoul **(0)2**, Busan **(0)51**.
The code to fax the UK from Korea is **00 44**.

Do you have a fax? 팩스 있어요?
p'ek-su issoyo?

I want to send 팩스를 보내고 싶어요
   a fax p'ek-su-rul ponego sip'oyo

What is your 팩스 번호가 뭐예요?
   fax number? p'ek-su ponho-ga mwo-yeyo?

My fax number 제 팩스 번호는 ... 예요
   is... che p'ek-su ponho-nun ... yeyo

Practicalities

Money

Cash dispensers work all day. Most banks are open from around 9.00 am to 5.00 pm (Monday to Friday). The **won** is the currency of Korea. Korea still very much operates on cash and sometimes it is problematic to find a place to use traveller's cheques and/or exchange currency. It is easier to change money at the airport or hotel.

신용 카드 shin-yong k'a-du	credit card
현금인출기 hyon-gum inch'ul-gi	cash dispenser
영수증 yong-soo-jung	till receipt

Where can I change some money?	어디서 환전 가능해요? odiso hwanjon kanung-haeyo?

When does the bank open?	은행은 언제 열어요?
	un-heng-un onje yoroyo?
When does the bank close?	은행은 언제 닫아요?
	un-heng-un onje tadayo?
Can I pay with...?	...으로 내도 돼요?
	...uro naedo tweyo?
won	원
	won
dollar	달러
	tal-la
pound	파운드
	p'a-un-du
I want to change these traveller's cheques	여행자 수표를 환전하고 싶어요
	yo-heng-ja soo-p'yo-rul hwanjon hago sip'oyo
Where is the nearest cash dispenser?	가까운 현금인출기는 어디 있어요?
	kakkaun hyongum inch'ul-gi-nun odi issoyo?
Can I use my credit card at the cash dispenser?	현금인출기에서 신용 카드 사용할 수 있어요?
	hyongum inch'ul-gi-eso shin-yong k'a-du sayong hal-soo issoyo?
Do you have any loose change?	잔돈 있어요?
	chandon issoyo?

Money

95

Paying

계산서	kesanso	**bill**
청구서	ch'ongguso	**invoice**
영수증	yong-soo-jung	**receipt**

How much is it?	얼마예요?
	olma-yeyo?
How much will it be?	얼마나 될까요?
	olmana twel-kkayo?
Can I pay by...?	...로 내도 돼요?
	...ro naedo tweyo?
credit card	신용카드
	shin-yong k'a-du
cheque	수표
	soo-p'yo
Is service included?	봉사료가 포함돼 있어요?
	pongsaryo-ga p'oham twe issoyo?
Is tax included?	세금 포함돼 있어요?
	segum p'oham twe issoyo?
Put it on my bill	계산서에 포함해 주세요
	kesanso-e p'oham hae chuseyo
Where do I pay?	어디서 지불해요?
	odiso chibul haeyo?

I need a receipt, please	영수증 부탁합니다 yong-soo-jung poot'ak'amnida
Do I pay in advance?	선불이에요? sonbul-iyeyo?
Do I need to pay a deposit?	보증금이 필요해요? pojung-gum-i p'iryo haeyo?
I'm sorry	미안합니다 mian-hamnida
I've nothing smaller	잔돈이 없어요 chandon-i opssoyo

YOU MAY HEAR...

부가세는 포함돼 있어요 pugase-nun p'oham twe issoyo	VAT is included
부가세는 포함돼 있지만 봉사료는 별도입니다 pugase-nun p'oham twe ichiman pongsaryo-nun pyotto imnida	VAT is included but not a service charge
계산대에서 지불해 주세요 kesande-eso chibul hae chuseyo	Pay at the till

Luggage

....

카트 katu | trolley

My luggage hasn't arrived
내 짐이 안 도착했어요
nae chim-i an toch'ak'hessoyo

My suitcase has been damaged on the flight
내 여행 가방이 비행 도중 손상됐어요
nae yohaeng kabang-i pihaeng tojung sonsang twessoyo

Repairs

....

Repairs while you wait
기다리시는 동안 해드립니다
kidarisinun dongan haedripnida

This is broken
이게 망가졌어요
ige mang-ga-jyossoyo

Where can I have this repaired?
어디서 수리가 가능해요?
odiso soori-ga kanung-haeyo?

Is it worth repairing?
수리할 가치가 있어요?
soori hal kach'i-ga issoyo?

> **Train** (p 34) > **Air travel** (p 42)

Can you repair...?	...수리 가능해요?
	...soori kanung-haeyo?
this	이거
	igo
these shoes	이 구두
	i kudu
my watch	내 시계
	nae shige

YOU MAY HEAR...

미안하지만, 수리할 수 없어요.	Sorry, but we can't mend it
mianhajiman, soori hal-soo opssoyo	

Repairs

> **Breakdown** (p 50)

Laundry

드라이크리닝 tu-rai-k'u-ri-ning	dry-cleaner's
세제 seje	soap powder
표백제 p'yobek-che	bleach
세탁기 se-t'ak-ki	washing machine

Where can I wash these clothes? 어디서 옷 세탁이 가능해요?
odiso ot set'a-gi kanung-haeyo?

Where is the nearest launderette? 제일 가까운 세탁소가 어디예요?
cheil kakkaun set'ak-so-ga odi-yeyo?

Complaints

The... does/ do not work (for machines) ...작동 안 해요
...chak-tong an haeyo

heating 난방이
nanbang-i

air conditioning	에어컨이
	e-o-k'on-i
The ... is/	...이/가 더러워요
are dirty	...i/ga torowoyo
toilet	화장실(이)
	hwajang-sil (i)
sheets	시트(가)
	shi-t'u (ga)
The light is not	전기가 안 들어와요
working	chon-gi-ga an turo-wayo
It's broken	망가졌어요
	mang-ga-jyossoyo
I want a refund	환불해 주세요
	hwanbul hae chuseyo

Problems

Can you help me?	도와 주시겠어요?
	towa chusigessoyo?
I speak very	한국말 잘 못해요
little Korean	hang-goong-mal chal mot' heyo
Does anyone here	누가 영어 할 수 있어요?
speak English?	nuga yong-o hal-soo issoyo?

> **Hotel desk** (p 56)

What's the matter?	무슨 일이에요?
	musun iri -yeyo?
I would like to speak to whoever is in charge...	...담당자에게 말하고 싶어요
	...tamdang-ja-ege mal-hago sip'oyo
I'm lost	길을 잃어버렸어요
	kirul iro poryossoyo
How do you get to...	...에 어떻게 가요?
	...e ottok'e kayo?
I missed my train	기차를 놓쳤어요
	kich'a-rul no-ch'yo-ssoyo
I missed my plane	비행기를 놓쳤어요
	piheng-gi-rul no-ch'yo-ssoyo
I missed my bus	버스를 놓쳤어요
	posu-rul no-ch'yo-ssoyo
I've missed my flight because there was an accident	사고가 나서 비행기를 놓쳤어요
	sago-ga naso piheng-gi-rul no-ch'yossoyo
The coach has left without me	버스가 출발해 버렸어요
	posu-ga ch'ulbal hae poryossoyo
Can you show me how this works, please?	사용하는 방법을 가르쳐 주시겠어요?
	sayong-hanun pang-bop-ul karuch'yo chusigessoyo?

I have lost my money	돈을 잃어 버렸어요
	ton-ul iro poryossoyo
I need to get to...	...에 꼭 가야 돼요
	...e kkok kaya tweyo
I need to get in touch with the British consulate	영국 영사관에 연락을 해야 돼요
	yong-guk yongsagwan-e yolla-gul haeya tweyo
Leave me alone!	혼자 있게 해 주세요!
	honja it-ke hae chuseyo!
Go away!	저리 가세요!
	chori kaseyo!

Emergencies

구급차	kugup-ch'a	ambulance
헌병	hon-pyong	military police
경찰	kyong-ch'al	police
소방관	sobang-kwan	firemen
소방대	sobang-de	fire brigade
경찰서	kyongch'al-so	police station

Help!	도와주세요!
	towa chuseyo!
Fire!	불이야!
	poo-ri-ya!
Can you help me?	도와 주시겠어요?
	towa chusigessoyo?
There's been an accident!	사고가 났어요!
	sago-ga nassoyo!
Someone...	누군가가...
	nugunga-ga...
has been injured	부상을 당했어요
	pusang-ul tang-hessoyo
has been knocked down	기절했어요
	kijol-hessoyo
Please call...	...을/를 불러 주세요
	...ul/rul pollo chuseyo
the police	경찰(을)
	kyong-ch'al (ul)
an ambulance	구급차(를)
	kugup-ch'a (rul)
Where is the police station?	경찰서가 어디에요?
	kyongch'al-so-ga odi-yeyo?
I want to report a crime	범죄 신고를 하고 싶어요
	pom-jwe sin-go-rul hago sip'oyo

I've been...	저는…
	cho-nun...
robbed	도둑 맞았어요
	toduk majassoyo
attacked	습격당했어요
	sup-kyok tang-hessoyo
Someone's stolen my bag	내 가방을 도둑 맞았어요
	nae kabang-ul toduk majassoyo
Someone's stolen my traveller's cheques	여행자 수표를 도둑 맞았어요
	yoheng-ja soop'yo-rul toduk majassoyo
My car has been broken into	자동차에 도둑이 들었어요
	chadong-ch'a-e todu-gi turossoyo
I've been raped	강간당했어요
	kang-gan tang-hessoyo
I want to speak to a policewoman	여자 경찰관하고 말하고 싶어요
	yoja kyongch'algwan-hago mal-hago sip'oyo
I need to make a telephone call	전화하고 싶어요
	chon-hwa-hago sip'oyo
I need a report for my insurance	보험회사에 낼 증명서가 필요해요
	poheom hwesa-e nel chung-myong-so-ga piro-heyo

105

I didn't know there was a speed limit	속도 제한이 있는 거 몰랐어요
	sok-to chehan-i innun go mol-lassoyo
How much is the fine?	벌금이 얼마예요?
	polgum-i olma-yeyo?
Where do I pay it?	어디에 지불해요?
	odi-e chibul haeyo?
Do I have to pay it straightaway?	즉시 내야 돼요?
	chuk-ssi neya tweyo?
I'm very sorry, officer	정말 미안합니다
	chong-mal mianhamnida

Health

Pharmacy

··

| 약국   yak-kuk | pharmacy/chemist |

Can you give me something for...?	...에 먹는 약 좀 주시겠어요? ...e mong-nun yak chom chushi-gessoyo?
a headache	두통 tu-t'ong
car sickness	차멀미 ch'a molmi
a cough	기침 kichim
diarrhoea	설사 sol-sa
Is it safe for children?	이거 아이들도 먹을 수 있어요? igo ai-dul-do mogul soo issoyo?
How much should I give him?	얼마나 먹어야 돼요? olmana mogoya tweyo?

하루에 3회 haru-e sam-hwe	Three times a day
식전 shik-chon	before meals
식후 shik'oo	after meals

Body

. . . .

In Korean the possessive (my, his, her, etc.) is not generally used when referring to parts of the body.

I've broken my leg	다리가 부러졌어요 tari-ga puro-jyossoyo
Mr Kim hurt his arm	김 선생님이 팔이 아파요 kim sonseng-nim-i p'ari ap'ayo

Health

108

Doctor

• •

| 병원 | pyong-won | hospital |
| 응급 | ung-kup | emergency |

FACE TO FACE

A 몸이 안 좋아요
mom-i an choayo
I feel ill

B 열이 있어요?
yori issoyo?
Do you have a temperature?

A 아니요, ...가 아파요
anio, ... ga ap'ayo
No, I have a pain here...

I need a doctor	의사를 불러 주세요
	ui-sa-rul pulo-juseyo
My son is ill	아들 아이가 아파요
	adul ai-ga ap'ayo
My daughter is ill	딸 아이가 아파요
	ttal ai-ga ap'ayo
I'm diabetic	당뇨병이 있어요
	tang-nyo-pyong-i issoyo

I'm pregnant	임신중이예요
	im-shin-jung i yeyo
I'm on the pill	피임 약을 먹고 있어요
	piim ya-gul mok-ko issoyo
I'm allergic to	페니실린 알레르기가 있어요
penicillin	penisirin al-le-ru-gi-ga issoyo
Will he/she have	(저/사람) 병원에 가야 돼요?
to go to	(cho/saram) pyong-won kaya
hospital?	tweyo?
When are visiting	방문 시간은 언제예요?
hours?	pangmun shigan-un onje-yeyo?
Will I have to pay?	돈 내야 돼요?
	ton neya tweyo?
How much will	얼마에요?
it cost?	olma-yeyo?
Can you give me	보험 받을 영수증 부탁합니다
a receipt for the	pohom padul yong-soo-jung
insurance?	poot'ak'amnida

병원에 가야 돼요 pyong-won-e kayo tweyo	You will have to go to hospital
걱정할 필요 없어요/ kok-chong hal piro opsoyo	You don't need to worry
큰 일 아니예요 k'un il ani-yeyo	It's not serious

Dentist

I need a dentist	치과에 가야 돼요 ch'i-kwa-e kayo tweyo
I have a toothache	이가 아파요 i-ga ap'ayo
Can you do a temporary filling?	임시로 봉해도 돼요? im-shi-ro pong hedo tweyo?
It hurts	아파요 ap'ayo
Can you give me something for the pain?	통증에 먹는 약 있어요? t'ong-chung-e mong-nun yak issoyo?

Dentist

> **Emergencies** (p 103)

Can you repair my dentures?	의치를 치료해 주세요 ui-ch'i-rul ch'iryo hae chuseyo
Do I have to pay?	돈 내야 돼요? ton neya tweyo?
How much will it be?	얼마예요? olma-yeyo?
Can I have a receipt for my insurance?	보험 받을 영수증 부탁합니다 pohom padul yong-soo-jung poot'ak'amnida

YOU MAY HEAR...

뽑아야 돼요 ppo-ba-ya tweyo	I'll have to take it out
봉해야 돼요 pong heya tweyo	You need a filling
조금 아플 거예요 chogum ap'ul ko-yeyo	This might hurt a little

Health

> **Pharmacy** (p 107)

Different types of travellers

Disabled travellers

. . . .

What facilities do you have for disabled people?
장애 자용 시설이 있어요?
chang-e-ja-yong shiso-ri issoyo?

Are there any toilets for the disabled?
장애 자용 화장실 있어요?
chang-e-ja-yong hwajangshi-ri issoyo?

Do you have any bedrooms on the ground floor?
일층에 방 있어요?
il-ch'ung-e pang issoyo?

Is there a lift?
엘리베이터 있어요?
el-li-be-i-t'o issoyo?

Where is the lift?
엘리베이터 어디 있어요?
el-li-be-i-t'o odi issoyo?

Can you visit ... in a wheelchair?
...은 휠체어로 방문 가능해요?
...un hwil-ch'e-o-ro pangmun kanung haeyo?

Do you have wheelchairs?	휠체어 있어요? hwil-ch'e-o issoyo?
Where is the wheelchair-accessible entrance?	휠체어용 출입구 있어요? hwil-ch'e-o-yong ch'urip-ku issoyo?
Is there a reduction for disabled people?	장애자 할인 돼요? chang-e-ja harin tweyo?
Is there somewhere I can sit down?	어디 앉을 데 있어요? odi anjul te issoyo?

With kids

Public transport is free for up to two non-school-children (normally) under 6 years old when travelling with an adult. Children between the ages of 7 and 12 pay half price. Most tourist places give child and student discounts.

> **Hotel desk** (p 56)

A child's ticket	어린이 표
	ori-ni p'yo
This child is ... years old	이 아이는 ... 살이예요
	i ai-nun ... sa-ri-yeyo
Is there a reduction for children?	어린이 할인 있어요?
	ori-ni harin issoyo?
Do you have a children's menu?	어린이용 메뉴 있어요?
	ori-ni-yong me-nyu issoyo?
Is it OK to take children?	어린이 동반 가능해요?
	ori-ni pongban kanung haeyo?
Do you have...?	... 있어요?
	...issoyo?
a high chair	하이체어
	ha-i-ch'e-o
a cot	유아용 침대
	yu-a-yong ch'imde
I have two children	아이가 둘 있어요
	ai-ga tul issoyo
This child is 8 years old	이 아이는 여덟살이예요
	i ai-nun yodol sari-yeyo
Do you have any children?	아이가 있어요?
	ai-ga issoyo?

With kids

> **Pharmacy** (p 107) > **Doctor** (p 109)

Reference

Alphabet

....

Consonants

....

Letter	Symbol
ㄱ	k
ㄴ	n
ㄷ	t
ㄹ	r/l
ㅁ	m
ㅂ	p
ㅅ	s/sh
ㅇ	ng
ㅈ	ch
ㅊ	ch'
ㅋ	k'
ㅌ	t'
ㅍ	p
ㅎ	h

Vowels

Letter	Symbol
ㅏ	a'
ㅑ	ya
ㅓ	ŏ
ㅕ	yŏ
ㅗ	o
ㅛ	yo
ㅜ	oo
ㅠ	yoo
ㅡ	u
ㅣ	i

Measurements and quantities

• •

1 lb = approx. 0.5 kilo   1 pint = approx. 0.5 litre

Liquid

1/2 litre of...	...반 리터
	...pan li-t'o
a litre of...	...일 리터
	...il li-t'o...
a bottle of...	...한 병
	... han pyong
a glass of...	...한 잔
	... han chan

Weights

100 grams	백 그램
	pek gu-rem
1/2 kilo of...	...오백 그램
	...o-pek gu-rem
a kilo of...	...일 킬로
	... il k'il-lo

Food

a slice of...	...한 조각
	... han chogak
a portion of...	...일인분
	... i-rin-bun
a dozen...	...한 타스
	...han t'a-su
a box of...	...한 상자
	... han sang-ja
a packet of...	...한 봉지
	... han pong-ji
a tin of.../	...캔 하나 (맥주) /
a can of...(beer)	...(mekju) ken hana
a jar of...	...한 병
	...han pyong

Miscellaneous

...won worth of...	...원 어치...
	...won o-ch'i...
a quarter	사분의 일
	sa-bun-e il
20 per cent	이십 퍼센트
	i-ship p'o-sen-t'u

more than...	...이상
	... i-sang
less than...	...이하
	... i-ha
double	두 배
	too pe
twice	두 번
	too pon

Numbers

There are two sets of cardinal numbers in Korean, native Korean numbers and numbers borrowed from Chinese (Chinese derived numbers).

Which set of numbers is used depends on what you are counting: Chinese derived numbers are used, for example, for minutes, metric weights and measures, dates (years, months, days), sums of money, addresses, phone numbers and numbers above 100.

Native Korean numbers are used, for example, for hours, a person's age, general counting of smaller numbers, etc.

However, it should still be clear what you mean even if you use one type of number where you should use the other.

Also, in Korean, numbers are used with counters (in other words, a category to which it belongs) such as - 장 ... chang ... for a thin flat object, or 송이 song-i ... for flowers. If you don't know which counter to use, you can use the general counter 개 ... gae instead.

	Chinese-derived form		Original Korean form	
0	영 / 공	yong/kong		
1	일	il	하나	hana
2	이	i	둘	tool
3	삼	sam	셋	set
4	사	sa	넷	net
5	오	o	다섯	tasot
6	육	yuk	여섯	yosot
7	칠	ch'il	일곱	ilgop
8	팔	p'al	여덟	yodol
9	구	koo	아홉	ahop
10	십	ship	열	yol

11	십일	ship-il	열하나	yol hana
12	십이	ship-i	열둘	yol dul
13	십삼	ship-sam	열셋	yol set
14	십사	ship-sa	열넷	yol net
15	십오	ship-o	열다섯	yol tasot
16	십육	ship-yuk	열여섯	yol yosot
17	십칠	ship-ch'il	열일곱	yol ilgop
18	십팔	ship-p'al	열여덟	yol yodol
19	십구	ship-koo	열아홉	yol ahop
20	이십	i-ship	스물	sumul
21	이십일	iship-il	스물하나	sumul hana
22	이십이	iship-i	스물둘	sumul tool
23	이십삼	iship-sam	스물셋	sumul set
24	이십사	iship-sa	스물넷	sumul net
25	이십오	iship-o	스물다섯	sumul tasot
26	이십육	iship-yuk	스물여섯	sumul yosot
27	이십칠	iship-ch'il	스물일곱	sumul ilgop
28	이십팔	iship-p'al	스물여덟	sumul yodol
29	이십구	iship-koo	스물아홉	sumul ahop
30	삼십	sam-ship	서른	sorun
40	사십	sa-ship	마흔	mahun
50	오십	o-ship	쉰	shin
60	육십	yuk-ship	예순	yesun
70	칠십	ch'il-ship	일흔	ilhun
80	팔십	p'al-ship	여든	yodun
90	구십	koo-ship	아흔	ahun

Beyond 100, only the Chinese-derived form is used

100	백	pek
110	백십	pek-ship
1000	천	ch'on
2000	이천	i-ch'on
10000	만	man
million	백만	pek-man
billion	십억	ship-ok

| 1st | 첫째 | 2nd | 둘째 |
| | ch'ot-cche | | tool-cche |

| 3rd | 셋째 | 4th | 넷째 |
| | set-cche | | net-cche |

| 5th | 다섯째 | 6th | 여섯째 |
| | tasot-cche | | yosot-cche |

| 7th | 일곱째 | 8th | 여덟째 |
| | ilgop-cche | | yodol-cche |

| 9th | 아홉째 | 10th | 열째 |
| | ahp-cche | | yol-cche |

Numbers

123

Days and months

●●●●●●●●●●●●●●●●●●●●●●●●●●●●●●●●●●●●●●

Days

Monday	월요일	wor-yoil
Tuesday	화요일	hwa-yoil
Wednesday	수요일	soo-yoil
Thursday	목요일	mok-yoil
Friday	금요일	kum-yoil
Saturday	토요일	t'o-yoil
Sunday	일요일	ir-yoil

Months

January	일월	ir-wol
February	이월	i-wol
March	삼월	sam-wol
April	사월	sa wol
May	오월	o-wol
June	유월	yu-wol
July	칠월	ch'ir-wol
August	팔월	p'al-wol
September	구월	koo-wol

October	시월	shi-wol
November	십일월	shipil-wol
December	십이월	shipi-wol

Seasons

spring	봄	pom
summer	여름	yorum
autumn	가을	kaul
winter	겨울	kyo-ool

What is today's date?	오늘 며칠이에요? onul myoch'i-ri-yeyo?
What day is it today?	오늘 무슨 요일이에요? onul musun yoil-i yeyo?
It's the 5th of March 2007	이천칠년 삼월 오일이에요 i-ch'on-ch'il-nyon sam-wol o-il i yeyo
on Saturday	토요일에 t'o-yoil-e
on Saturdays/ every Saturday	매주 토요일에 meju t'o-yoil-e
this Saturday	이번 토요일 ibon t'o-yoil
next Saturday	다음 토요일 taum t'o-yoil

last Saturday	지난 토요일
	chi-nan t'o-yoil
in June	유월에
	yu-wol-e
at the beginning of June	유월초에
	yu-wol-ch'o-e
at the end of June	유월말에
	yu-wol-mal-e
before summer	여름 전에
	yorum chon-e
during the summer	여름에
	yorum-e
after summer	여름 후에
	yorum hoo-e

Time

What time is it, please?	지금 몇시예요?
	chigum myo-ssi-yeyo?
a.m.	오전
	ojon
p.m.	오후
	o-hoo

2 o'clock	두 시
	too shi
3 o'clock	세 시
	se shi
It's 1 o'clock	한 시예요
	han shi-yeyo
It's midday	정오예요
	chong-o-yeyo
It's midnight	자정이예요
	chajong-i yeyo
9	아홉시
	ahop shi
9.10	아홉시 십분
	ahop shi ship pun
quarter past 9	아홉시 십오분
	ahop shi ship-o pun
9.20	아홉시 이십분
	ahop shi iship pun
half past 9	아홉시 반
	ahop shi pan
9.35	아홉시 삼십오분
	ahop shi samship-o pun
quarter to 10	열시 십오분 전
	yol shi ship-o pun chon
5 minutes to 10	열시 오분 전
	yol shi o pun chon

127

Time phrases

....

When does it open?	언제 열어요? onje yoroyo?
When does it close?	언제 닫아요? onje tadayo?
When does it begin?	언제 시작해요? onje shijak'eyo?
When does it finish?	언제 끝나요? onje kkunnayo?
at 3 o'clock	세 시에 se shi-e
before 3 o'clock	세 시 전에 se shi jon-e
after 3 o'clock	세 시 이후에 se shi i-hoo-e
today	오늘 onul
tonight	오늘밤 onul pam
tomorrow	내일 nae-il
yesterday	어제 o-je

Reference

Eating out

Food in Korea

All types of eating places and food can be found in Korea. Except for in hotel restaurants and up-market traditional Korean restaurants, which usually have set dining times, you can have your meal at any time throughout the day. American style fast food is popular and there are family restaurants that cater for this. There are also many specialized restaurants where only one type of food is served. Visit **www.knto.or.kr** for a guide to eating out in Korea.

Most coffee shops and restaurants will automatically bring you a glass of tap water (which is safe to drink). In traditional Korean restaurants you will find low tables and (often) **pangseok** 방석 (a floor cushion). These restaurants require you to remove your shoes so make sure your socks are respectable.

Food in Korea

Service charge/Tax and tip

A VAT and a 10% service charge are generally
included in the bill and tipping is not customary.

Bill

The word for the bill is '**Kesanso**'. You can ask for
the bill by saying 'Kesanso poot'ak'amnida'.

Coffee shops 다방 / 커피숍 (tabang/k'o-p'i-shop)

Coffee shops serve non-alcoholic drinks and many
of them also serve food such as salads, sandwiches,
pasta dishes and rice dishes. If you would like to
order tea with milk, be sure to specify **milku ti**, as
otherwise you will probably be served a lemon tea.

Noodle shops
국수집 / 분식점 (kuk-soo-chip/punshik-chom)

Noodles are very popular and cheap in Korea.
There are many types of noodles available: **udong**,
buckwheat and **raamyon**. You can choose
different toppings such as chicken or **kimchi**

(a strongly flavoured fermented cabbage pickle, similar to sauerkraut, but made from Chinese cabbage and seasoned with garlic, chilli and salt, etc.). **Raamyon** originated in China but has gained huge popularity amongst all generations in Korea.

Pubs 생맥주집 (seng-mek-chu chip)

Seng-mek-chu is draft beer and pubs are very good places to try out a range of beers and drinks. They serve cheap but very tasty food in small portions, and usually have a large selection to choose from.

Family restaurants
패밀리 레스토랑 (famili restorang)

There are many chain family restaurants where you can have different types of food. They are often located on major roads.

Vending machines
자동판매기 (chadong p'an-me-gi)

Vending machines contain all kinds of hot and cold drinks as well as snacks. Notes can be used in the machines.

Department stores 백화점 (p'e-k'wa-jom)

Most department stores have a designated restaurant floor where you will find various types of restaurant, including western style. These are good places to visit to familiarize yourself with the kind of food you can get in Korea. Department store basement floors have good delis and take-away food.

FACE TO FACE

A 주문하시겠어요?
chumun hashigessoyo?
May I have your order?

B 밀크티 부탁합니다
mil-k'u t'i poot'ak'amnida
A tea with milk, please

a coffee	커피
	k'o-p'i
a beer	맥주
	mek-chu
a lemon squash	레몬 스쿼시
	remon su-k'wo'shi
tea	차
	cha
with lemon	레몬
	remon
sugar	설탕
	sol-t'ang
for two	두 사람
	too saram
for me	저는
	cho-nun
for him/her	저 분은
	cho pun-un
for us	우리는
	oo-ri-nun
with ice	얼음하고
	orum-hago
a bottle of	생수 한 병
mineral water	seng-soo han pyong

sparkling	탄산수
	t'an-san-soo
still	물
	mul

Other drinks to try

냉커피 neng-k'o-p'i **iced coffee**

녹차 nok-ch'a **green tea**. This is the tea used for tea ceremonies in Korean temples. It is very mild

보리차 pori-ch'a **barley tea**. This is usually served with your meal for free in Korean restaurants

홍차 hongcha **red tea**

레몬차 lemoncha **lemon tea**

FACE TO FACE

A ...사람 자리를 예약하고 싶어요
...saram chari-rul yeyak'go sip'oyo
I'd like to book a table for ... people

B 네, 언제요?
ne, onjeyo?
Yes, when for?

A 오늘밤...
onul pam...
for tonight...

The menu, please	메뉴 부탁합니다 me-nyu poot'ak'amnida
What is the dish of the day?	오늘의 특별 요리는 뭐예요? onur-e t'ul-pyol yori-nun mwo-yeyo?
Do you have a tourist menu?	여행자용 메뉴도 있어요? yoheng-ja-yong me-nyu-do issoyo?
What is the speciality of the house?	이 식당의 추천 요리는 뭐예요? i shik-tang-e ch'u-ch'on yori-nun mwo-yeyo?
Can you tell me what this is?	이게 뭐예요? ige mwo-yeyo?
I'll have this	이거 주세요 igo chuseyo
Could we have some more bread, please?	빵 좀 더 주세요 ppang/mool chom to chuseyo
Could we have some more water, please?	물 좀 더 주세요 mool chom to chuseyo
The bill, please	계산서 부탁합니다 kesan-so poot'ak'amnida
Is service included?	봉사료가 포함돼 있어요? pongsaryo-ga p'oham twe issoyo?

135

Vegetarian

• •

The majority of restaurants do not indicate
vegetarian food but there are always some
vegetarian dishes on the menu. Don't hesitate to
tell the staff that you are a vegetarian and what you
can and cannot eat; they will be happy to advise you
on suitable dishes.

I am a vegetarian	저는 채식주의자예요
	cho-nun ch'eshik-chu-i-ja-yeyo
I don't eat meat	고기를 안 먹어요
	kogi-rul an mogoyo
I don't eat meat and fish	고기하고 생선을 안 먹어요
	kogi-hago seng-son-ul an mogoyo
Are there any vegetarian restaurants here?	여기 채식식당 있어요?
	yogi ch'e-shik shik-tang issoyo?
Do you have any vegetarian dishes?	채식메뉴 있어요?
	ch'e-shik me-nyu issoyo?
Which dishes have no meat?	고기 안 들어간 음식이 있어요?
	kogi an turo-gan umshil issoyo?

Which dishes have no fish?	생선 안 들어간 음식이 있어요?	seng-son an turo-gan umshil issoyo?
What fish dishes do you have?	무슨 생선 요리가 있어요?	musun seng-son yori-ga issoyo?
What do you recommend?	뭘 추천하시겠어요?	mwol ch'u-ch'on hasigessoyo?
I'd like rice as a main course	메인 코스로 밥을 주세요	me-in k'o-su-ro pabul chuseyo
I don't like meat	고기를 안 좋아해요	kogi-rul an choa-heyo
Egg is all right	달걀은 괜찮아요	tal-gyal-un kwen-ch'anayo
Is it made with vegetable stock?	이거 야채 스프로 만든거예요?	igo yache-supu-ro mandun go yeyo?

Wines and spirits

•••••••••••••••••••••••••••••••••••••••

포도주 podoju wine
막걸리 makgeolli unrefined rice wine
청주 cheongju refined rice wine
소주 soju alcoholic drink made from rice and other
　ingredients such as wheat, barley, sweet potato or
　tapioca.
동동주 tong-dong-ju Korean rice wine. There are
　different degrees of sweetness and lots of local
　ones.
매실주 me-sil-chu Korean plum wine. It is smooth
　and sweet and popular among women.
인삼주 insamju ginseng wine

The wine list, please	와인 메뉴 부탁합니다 wa-in me-nyu poot'ak'amnida
white wine	화이트 와인 hwaitu wain
red wine	레드 와인 redu wain
Can you recommend a good local wine?	좋은 와인 추천해 　주시겠어요? choun wa-in ch'u-ch'on hae 　　chusigessoyo?

A bottle...	...한 병
	...han pyong
of house wine	하우스 와인
	ha-oo-su wain
What liqueurs do you have?	무슨 술이 있어요?
	musun soo-ri issoyo?

Menu reader

아구찜 agujjim steamed spicy angler fish

알탕 altang spicy fish egg soup

안심구이 anshim-gui grilled beef tenderloin

밥 bap rice (cooked)

버섯 beoseot mushroom

버섯볶음 beoseot bokkeum sautéed mushroom salad

비빔냉면 bibim naengmyon spicy buckwheat noodles

비빔밥 bibimbap steamed rice mixed with vegetables, egg and chilli paste

비빔국수 bibimguksu noodles mixed with hot pepper paste

빈대떡 bin dae tteok mung bean pancake

볶음밥 bokgeumbap fried rice

보신탕 bosin-tang dog soup

보쌈 bossam steamed pork and cabbage

북어국 bugeo-guk pollock soup

불고기 bulgogi barbecued beef

불갈비 bulgalbi grilled ribs

철판구이 cheolpan gui grilled beef, seafood and
  vegetables

추어탕 chueo-tang loach soup

대합 daehap clam

닭갈비 dak galbi grilled spicy chicken and
  vegetables

닭구이 dak-gui grilled chicken

닭백숙 dakbaeksuk steamed chicken

닭고기 dakgogi chicken

닭찜 dakjjim chicken stew

떡국 ddeok-guk rice cake soup

더덕구이 deodeok-gui grilled toduk root

등심구이 deungshim-gui grilled sirloin

된장찌개 doenjang-jjigae soya bean paste stew

도가니탕 dogani-tang knuckle bone soup

돌솥비빔밥 dolsot bibimbap mixed vegetables
  served on rice

도라지나물 doraji namul bellflower root salad

두부찌개 dubujjigae tofu stew

돼지고기 dwaejigogi pork

돼지갈비 dwaejigalbi roasted pork ribs

가지나물 gaji namul steamed aubergine salad

갈비 galbi pork or beef ribs

갈비구이 galbi-gui grilled beef ribs
갈비찜 galbijjim beef rib stew
갈비탕 galbi-tang beef rib soup
감자 gamja potato
감자탕 gamjatang potato soup
게 ge crab
꼬리곰탕 ggori gom-tang oxtail soup
김 gim dried seaweed
김밥 gimbap rice wrapped in seaweed
김치국 gimchiguk kimchi soup
고추 gochu red pepper, chilli
꼬리곰탕 gom-tang meat and tripe soup
공기밥 gonggibap boiled rice
곱창전골 gopchang-jeongol spicy beef tripe and
   vegetable stew
고사리나물 gosari namul parboiled bracken salad
국 / 탕 guk/tang soup
국수 guksu wheat flour noodles
굴 gul oyster
계란탕 gyeran-tang egg soup
해물탕 haemultang spicy seafood stew
해장국 haejang-guk (hangover soup) soup made
   with bones, meat, cabagge and blood
한정식 hanjeong sik Korean set meal

호박나물 hobak namul squash (pumpkin) leaves salad

회덮밥 hoe deop bap sliced raw fish salad

회냉면 hoe naengmyon buckwheat noodles with raw fish

장어구이 jangeo-gui grilled eel

잡채 japchae mixed vegetables with noodles

제육볶음 jeyukbokkeum spicy stir-fried pork with vegetables

짜장밥 jjajangbap rice with brown bean sauce

찌개 jjigae stew

쫄면 jjol-myeon chewy noodles mixed with fresh vegetables

족발 jokbal steamed pork hocks

죽 juk porridge

칼국수 kalguksu handmade noodles

김치 kimchi a strongly flavoured fermented cabbage pickle, a bit similar to sauerkraut, but usually made from Chinese cabbage and seasoned with garlic, chilli and salt etc.

배추김치 baechu kimchi Chinese cabbage kimchi

백김치 baek kimchi kimchi made without chilli

보쌈김치 bossam kimchi, fillings are wrapped with cabbage leaves

총각김치 chonggak kimchi young radish kimchi

동치미 dongchimi watery radish kimchi

깍두기 ggakdugi chopped radish kimchi

김치국 gimchiguk kimchi soup

김치볶은밥 kimchi bokkeumbap stir-fried rice made with kimchi

김치찌개 kimchi-jjiggae kimchi stew

나박김치 nabak kimchi thin-sliced radish and Chinese cabbage kimchi

열무물김치 yeolmumul kimchi summer green kimchi, watery kimchi using young radishes with leaves

콩 kong bean

콩나물 kongnamul bean sprout salad

콩나물국 kongnamul guk bean sprout soup

콩나물밥 kongnamulbap rice with bean sprouts

매운탕 maeun-tang hot spicy fish soup

막국수 makguksu buckwheat noodles with clear chicken soup

만두 mandu dumplings

만두국 mandu-guk dumpling soup

마늘 maneul garlic

마파두부밥 mapadubu deopbap rice with tofu and Chinese hot pepper

미역국 miyeok-guk brown seaweed soup

미역냉국 miyeoknaeng-guk seaweed soup in chilled vinegar water

면 / 국수 myeon/guksu noodles

무 mu radish

물냉면 mul naengmyon cold buckwheat noodles served in a large bowl with an iced broth

냉면 naengmyon cold buckwheat noodles

냉 콩국수 naengkongguksu noodles in soya bean water

낙지볶음밥 nakji bokkeumbap stir-fried octopus

낙지전골 nakji-jeongol octopus stew

오곡밥 ogokbap five-grain rice

오이 oi cucumber

오이냉국 oinaneng guk chilled cucumber salad

오징어 ojingeo cuttlefish

오징어덮밥 ojingeo deopbap rice with cuttlefish

파전 pajeon green onion pancake

보리차 poricha barley tea

라면 ramyeon instant noodles

생선 saaengseon fish

생선구이 saengseon-gui grilled fish

새우 saeu shrimp

새우튀김 saeu twigim deep-fried shrimp

삼계탕 samgye-tang ginseng chicken soup
삼겹살 구이 samgyeopsal-gui grilled side of pork
설렁탕 seolleong-tang ox bone soup
시금치 sigeumchi spinach
소금구이 sogeumgui grilled meat with salt
소고기 sogogi beef
소고기 전골 sogogi-jeongol beef and vegetable
    stew
쌀국수 ssalguksu rice noodle
숙주나물 sukju namul mung bean sprouts salad
순두부 sundubu soft tofu
순대 sundae Korean sausage
순두부찌개 sunubu-jjigae soft tofu stew
떡볶이 tteokbokki stir-fired rice cake
우동 udong Japanese noodles
양 곱창구이 yang gobchang-gui grilled mutton tripe
양고기 yanggoggi mutton
양파 yangpa onion
약밥 yakbap rice fruit cake
연근 yeonggeun lotus root
영양탕 yeongyang-tang dog soup
육개장 yukgaejang hot and spicy stew soup

Grammar

The most noticeable difference between Korean grammar and that of the Indo-European languages is the word order of a sentence. The basic Korean word order is Subject, Object, Verb whilst the word order of an English sentence is Subject, Verb, Object. Also there are no prepositions, but postpositions. For example, the word order 'I go to school' is 'I school to go' in Korean.

Another important factor in Korean grammar is honorifics. The speaker can show respect to the listener and/or to the person they are speaking about by using appropriate verb forms. They can also make themselves humble in the same way. It all depends on the relationship of the parties involved. For example, if the speaker is talking to their grandfather, the speaker may use the honorific forms, but the grandfather will use a lower form of speech to the speaker.

Also, subjects and objects are usually followed by an ending. They are: **i** and **ga** (이 and 가) for the subject, and **ul** and **rul** (을 and 를) for the object. Whether a word ends in a consonant or a vowel determines which ending is used.

There are two sets of numbers: Korean numbers and Sino-Korean numbers. The usage of these numbers is determined by custom. For example, to say '20 minutes past 1', the Sino-Korean number is used for 20 (minutes), but the Korean number is used for 1 (hour).

Another useful fact to know is that there is a dictionary form of verbs (infinitive). In sentences, this dictionary verb form is always conjugated appropriately.

There are also many homonyms (words which are pronounced and written the same, but have different meanings). Therefore, to know the meaning of a word, you often have to know the context.

Public holidays

1 January	New Year's Day
February (movable)	Lunar New Year's Day
1 March	Independence Movement Day
May (movable)	Buddha's Birthday
5 May	Children's Day
6 June	Memorial Day
17 July	Constitution Day
15 August	Independence Day
September (movable)	Thanksgiving Day
3 October	National Foundation Day
25 December	Christmas Day

Signs and notices

General

공중변소	kongjung pyonso	public toilet
금연	kum-yon	non-smoking
꺼요	kkoyo	to switch off
당기세요	tangiseyo	to pull
남자 화장실	namja hwajangshil	gents (toilet)
미세요	miseyo	to push
비상구	pisanggu	emergency exit
비어있는	pio innun	free (not occupied)
여자 화장실	yoja hwajang shil	ladies (toilet)
입구	ipku	entrance
입구	ip-ku	way in
출구	ch'ulgu	exit
출구	ch'ulgu	way out
켜요	k'yoyo	to switch on
화재 경보기	hwaje kyongbogi	fire alarm

Airport

게이트	ke-i-t'u	gate
공항	kong-hang	airport
공항버스	konghang-bo-su	airport bus
놓쳐요	noch'o-yo	to miss
도착	toch'ak	arrivals (airport)
면세	myonse	duty-free
비행기	piheng-gi	plane
비자	pi-ja	visa
비지니스 클래스	pijinisu k'ul-la-su	business class
수하물 수취대	soohamul sooch'wide	baggage reclaim
수하물 한도	soo-ha-mul hando	luggage allowance
세관	segwan	customs
세관 신고	segwan shin-go	customs declaration
여권	yo-kwon	passport
일반석	Ilbansok	economy class
연결편	yongyolp'yon	connection

일등석	iltungsok	first class
지연돼요	chiyon tweyo	to be delayed
초과 화물	ch'ogwa hwamul	excess baggage
출발	ch'ulbal	departures
출발 라운지	ch'ulbal la-un-ji	departure lounge
출입국관리소	ch'u-rip-kuk kwal-li-so	passport control
취소/캔슬	ch'wiso/k'en-sul	cancellation
탑승권	t'apsung-kwon	boarding pass
터미날	t'e-mi-nal	terminal

Railway station

객차	kekch'a	carriage
고속열차	kosok yolch'a	express train
기차	kich'a	train
목적지	mokchokchi	destination
수하물 보관소	soo-hamul po-gwanso	left luggage office
승강장	seunggangjang	platform

시간표	shiganp'yo	timetable
야행열차	yaheng yolch'a	overnight train
역	yok	station
연결편	yongyolp'yon	connection
왕복표	wangbok-p'yo	return ticket
직행	chik'eng	direct train
편도 티켓	p'yondo t'i-k'et	one-way ticket

In the carriage

객실	kekshil	compartment
금연차	kumyon ch'a	non-smoking compartment
식당차	shiktang-ch'a	restaurant car
이등석	itungsok	second class
일등석	iltungsok	first class
지정석	chijong-sok	reserved seat

Outside the station/ taxi stands

•••••••••••••••••••••••••••••••••

대형버스	taehyong po-su	coach
버스	po-su	bus
버스 정류소	po-su chongnyuso	bus stop
버스 터미날	po-su t'o-mi-nal	bus station
버스 터미날	po-su t'o-mi-nal	coach station
주차장	chuch'ajang	car park
주차장	chuch'a-jang	parking lot
택시	tekshi	taxi
택시 기사	t'ek-shi-gisa	taxi driver
택시 승차장	t'ek-shi sungch'ajang	taxi rank

On the street (places and related words)

• •

경찰서	kyongch'al-so	police station
게스트 하우스	ke-su-t'u-ha-u-su	guesthouse
수퍼마켓	su-p'o-ma-k'et	supermarket
여관	yogwan	Korean hotel
여행사	yohengsa	travel agent's
우체국	oo-ch'e-guk	post office
유스호스텔	yu-su-ho-su-t'el	youth hostel
인터넷 카페	in-t'o-net k'a-p'e	Internet café
주유소	chu-yu-so	petrol station
지하철	chihach'ol	underground (metro)
호텔	ho-t'el	hotel
호스텔	ho-su-t'el	hostel
환전소	hwanjonso	bureau de change

On the street (other road signs)

거리	kori	avenue
교차로	kyoch'aro	junction
교통	kyot'ong	traffic
교통체증	kyot'ong ch'ejung	traffic jam
길 / 도로	kil/toro	road
길 / 도로	kil/toro	street
남 (쪽)	nam (chok)	south
도로표지	toro p'yoji	road sign
동 (쪽)	tong(chok)	east
똑바로	ttok-pparo	straight on
북 (쪽)	puk (chok)	north
속도 제한	sok-to chehan	speed limit
서 (쪽)	so (chok)	west
시내 ; 도심	shinae; toshim	city centre
시내	shi-ne	town centre
신호등	shinhodung	traffic lights
십자로	shipcharo	crossroads
지역	chiyok	district
횡단보도	hweng-dan podo	pedestrian crossing
횡단보도	hwengdan podo	zebra crossing

Telephone

• •

공중전화	kong-joong chonhwa	payphone
장거리 전화	changgori chonhwa	long-distance call
전화박스	chonhwa pak-su	phone box
전화번호	chonhwa ponho	telephone number
전화번호부	chonhwa ponhobu	telephone directory
전화카드	chonhwa k'a-du	phonecard
전화해요	chohwa haeyo	to dial
카드용 전화	k'a-du yong chonhwa	cardphone
코인/동전	k'o-in/tongjon	coin
콜렉트 콜	kol-lek-t'u k'ol	reverse-charge call
통화중	t'onghwa jung	engaged (phone)

Hotel

....

더블 룸/	to-bul rum/	double room
이인용 방	iinyong pang	
룸서비스	rum so-bi-su	room service
리셉션 데스크	ri-sep-syon	reception
	de-su-k'u	(desk)
빈 방	pin pang	vacancy
식사 제공	shiksa chegong	full board
싱글룸,	singul rum,	single room
일인용 방	irinyong pang,	
안내원	annewon	receptionist
트윈 베드룸	t'u-win	twin-bedded
	be-du-rum	room
프론트	p'u-ron-t'u	check-in desk

Restaurant

• •

메뉴	me-nyu	menu
식당	shik-tang	restaurant
세트 메뉴	se-t'u menyu	set menu
셀프 서비스	sel-p'u so-bi-su	self-service
음료수	umnyo-soo	soft drink
저녁 식사/ 석식	chonyok shiksa/ sokshik	dinner
점심	chom-shim	lunch
코스 메뉴	k'o-su menyu	course (meal)

Sightseeing

가이드북	ka-i-du-book	guidebook
가이드 투어	ka-i-du-t'u-o	guided tour
관광	kwan-gwang	sightseeing
관광 안내소	kwangwang anneso	tourist office
노인	noin	senior citizen
박물관	pangmul-gwan	museum
안내서	an-ne-su	leaflet
안내소	anneso	information office
예약실	yeyakshil	booking office
입장료	ip-chang-nyo	admission fee
입장료	ipchangnyo	entrance fee
절	chol	Buddhist temple
매표소	mep'yoso	ticket office
투어 / 여행	t'u-o/yoheng	tour (sightseeing)
표	p'yo	ticket

Shops

....

닫혔어요 / 휴업	tachyessoyo/ hyu-op	closed (shops)
반값 / 반액	pan kap/panek	half-price
세일	se-il	sale (in shops)
신용카드	shinyong k'a-du	credit card
영수증	yong-soo-jung	receipt
탈의실	t'aluishil	fitting room
할인	harin	bargain
할인 / 디스카운트	harin/ ti-su-k'a-un-t'u	discount
환불	hwanbul	refund

At the bank

....

지점	chijom	branch
여행자 수표	yohengja soop'yo	traveller's cheque
은행	unheng	bank
현금 인출기	hyongum inchulki	cash dispenser
환율	hwannyul	exchange rate

English – Korean

English	Korean	Romanization
A		
a, an	1, 한, 하나	il, han, hana
abroad	해외 (에)	hewe(e)
accelerator	악세레터 / 가속 페달	ak-se-re-t'o/ kasok pedal
to accept	받아요	padayo (dic. patta)
do you accept credit cards?	신용 카드도 받아요?	shinyong k'a-du-do padayo?
accident (traffic, etc.)	사고	sago
accident and emergency department	응급실	ung-gup-shil
accommodation	숙소	suk-so
account (bank)	계좌	kyechwa
ache	아파요	ap'ayo
my head aches	머리 아파요	mori ap'ayo
adapter (electrical)	어댑터	o-dep-t'o
address	주소	chuso
admission fee	입장료	ip-chang-nyo
adult	어른 / 성인	orun/song-in
advance: in advance	미리	miri
advance payment	선불	sonbul
advertisement	선전 / 광고	sonjon/ kwang-go
to advise	조언하다	cho-on-hata

English	Korean	romanization
what do you advise?	어떻게 하면 좋을까요?	ottok'e hamyon cho-ulkkayo?
to afford: I can't afford it	너무 비싸요	nomu pissayo
afternoon	오후	o-hoo
in the afternoon	오후에	o-hoo-e
this afternoon	오늘 오후	onul-o-hoo
again	다시	tashi
age (person's)	나이	nai
(time)	시대	shide
agenda (for meeting)	안건	an-kkon
ago: a week ago	일주일 전	jjuil-jon

English	Korean	romanization
to agree (support a proposal):		
I agree	찬성합니다	ch'an-song-hamnida
I don't agree	반대합니다	pandae-hamnida
aid (charity)	도움	to-um
AIDS	에이즈	e-i-ju
air	공기	kong-gi
air conditioning	에어콘	e-o-k'on
air hostess	스튜어디스	su-t'yu-o-di-su
air pollution	공기 오염	kong-gi-o-yom
airline	항공사	hang-gongsa

162 | 163

English – Korean

English – Korean

airmail	항공우편	hang-gong-oop'yon	allowed: is it allowed?	괜찮아요? kwench'anayo?
airport	공항	kong-hang	alone	혼자 honja
airport bus	공항버스	konghang-bo-su	always	항상 hangsang
alarm (in bank, shop)	비상벨	pisang-bel	a.m. (before noon)	오전 ojon
alarm call	알람콜	al-lam-k'ol	ambulance	구급차 kugupch'a
alarm clock	자명종, 알람 cha-myongjong, alam		America	미국 miguk
alcohol	술	sol	American (adj)	미국 miguk
all	다	ta	American (person)	미국 사람 miguk saram
allergic: I'm allergic to shellfish	조개 알레르기 chogae allerugi 있어요 issoyo		anaesthetic	마취 약 mach'wiyak
			ancestor	조상 chosang
			ancient	옛날 yennal
			and (furthermore)	또 tto

English	Korean	romanization
and	그리고	kurigo
angry	화난	hwanan
animal	동물	tongmul
ankle	발목	palmok
anniversary	기념일	kinyomil
wedding anniversary	결혼 기념일	kyolhon kinyomil
another (a different kind)	다른 거	tarun go
I'd like *another*	다른 거 주세요	tarun go chuseyo
another (one more)	하나 더	hana to

English	Korean	romanization
answer	회신	hweshin
(written)	대답/응답	tedap/ungdap
(spoken)	자동응답기	chadong ung-dap-ki
answering machine		
antibiotic	항생제	hangsengje
antihistamine	항히스타민제	hang-hisut aminje
antiseptic	살균제 / 소독제	salgyunje/ sodosje
anyone	아무나	amuna
anything	아무것	amugŏt
anywhere	어디나	odina
apartment	아파트	a-pa-t'u

English – Korean   164 | 165

apologies:	죄송합니다!	chwesong hamnida!	to arrange:	만날 시간을	manal shiganul
my apologies! (formal)			can we arrange a meeting?	정할까요?	chonghal kkayo?
(informal)	미안해요	mianheyo	arrivals (airport)	도착	toch'ak
appendicitis	맹장염	mengjangyom	to arrive	도착해요	tocha k'eyo
appetite	밥맛 / 입맛	pammat/ immat			(dic. toch'ak'ada)
			art	미술	misul
apple	사과	sagwa	art gallery	미술관	misulgwan
apple juice	사과 쥬스	sagwa ju-su	arthritis	관절염	kwanjolyom
application (job)	신청	shinch'ong	artist	화가	hwaga
appointment	약속	yaksok	as: as soon as possible	가능한 빨리	kanunghan ppalli
April	4월	sa wol	ashtray	재떨이	chettori
are: are there any...?	...있어요?	...issoyo?	Asia	아시아	asia
arm	팔	p'al			

English	Korean	Romanization	English	Korean	Romanization
to ask	물어봐요	murobwayo (dic. muroboda)	audience (theatre, etc.)	관객	kwangek
asparagus	아스파라가스	asup'aragasu	August	팔월	p'al-wol
aspirin	아스피린	a-su-p'i-rin	aunt	아주머니	sukmo, ajumoni
do you have any aspirin?	아스피린 있어요?	asup'irin issoyo?	Australia	호주	hoju
assistant (shop)	점원/도우미	chomwon/toumi	Australian (adj)	호주(의)	hoju(e)
asthma	천식	ch'onshik	(person)	호주 사람	hoju saram
I get asthma	천식이 있어요	ch'onsigi issoyo	author	작가	chakka
at: at home	집에	chibe	automatic (car)	오토	oto
at 4 o'clock	네 시에	neshie	autumn	가을	kaul
atmosphere (of place)	분위기	punwigi	available: when will it be available?	언제 있어요?	onje issoyo?
			avalanche	산사태	sansat'e
attractive	예쁜	yeppun	avenue	거리	kori

English – Korean

English – Korean

away: I will be away in August	팔 월에 없을거예요	p'alwol-e opsulgo-yeyo
B		
baby	아기	agi
baby food	유아식	yuashik
baby milk	아기 우유	agi oo-yu
baby seat	유아석	yuasok
baby wipes	아기용	agiyong mool-soogon
	물수건	
back (of body)	등	tung
(adv) when will he be back?	언제 돌아와요?	cnje torawayo?

I'd like to go back	돌아가고 싶어요	toragago sip'oyo
bad (character, morally)	나쁜	nappun
(food)	상한 / 맛없는	sanghan/ madumnun
bag	가방	kabang
baggage	짐	chim
baggage reclaim	수하물 수취대	soohamul soochwidae
baker's	빵집 / 제과점	ppangch'ip/ chegwajom
ball	공	kong
band (musical)	밴드	ben-du
bandage	반창고	panch'anggo

bank	은행	unheng
bar (to drink in)	술집 / 바	soolchip/ba
bar of chocolate	초콜릿 가게	ch'o·k'o·let kage
barbecue	바베큐	pa·be·k'yu
barber's	이발소	ibalso
bargain	할인	harin
it's a bargain	가격이예요	harin kagyok-iyeyo
baseball	야구	yagu
baseball game	야구 시합	yagu shihap
basement	지하	chiha
basket	바구니	paguni
basketball	농구	nonggu
bath	목욕	mogyok

bath towel	수건	sugon
bath tub	욕조	yokcho
bathroom	목욕탕	mogyokt'ang
battery		
(for radio, etc.)	건전지	konjonji
(for car)	배터리	paetturi
beach	해변	hebyon
bean (soya)	콩	k'ong
beautiful	아름다운	arumdaun
how beautiful!	아주	aju
	아름다워요!	arumdawoyo!
bed	침대	ch'imde
double bed	더블 침대	to·bul ch'imde
single bed	싱글 침대	singgul ch'imde

168 | 169

English – Korean

English	Korean		English	Korean	
bed and breakfast	민박	m nbak	before next week	다음주 전	taumchu chon
bedding	침구	ch'imgu	to begin	시작해 요	shijak'eyo
bedroom	침실	ch'imshil			(dic. shijak'ada)
single (bedroom)	싱글 룸	singgul lum	to belong to:	내 것이에요	negoshiyeyo
double (bedroom)	더블 룸	tobul lum	it/they		
			belong(s) to me		
beef	소고기	sogogi	does this	당신 거예요?	tangshin go-
beer	맥주	mekchu	belong to you?		yeyo?
bottled beer	병맥주	pyong mekchu	belt	벨트	pel-t'u
draught beer	생맥주	seng mekchu	beside	앞에	yop'e
before	...전	...chon	can I sit	앞에 앉아도	yop'e anjado
before	네 시 전	ne shi chon	beside you?	돼 요?	tweyo?
4 o'clock			best: I like	이게 제일	ige cheil
			this best	좋아요	choayo

better	좋은	choun
bicycle	자전거	chajonge
big	큰	k'un
bigger	더 큰	to k'un
have you anything bigger?	더 큰 거 있어요?	to k'un go issoyo?
bike	자전거	chajonge
mountain	마운틴	ma-un-t'in
bike	바이크	ba-i-k'u
bill	계산서	kesanso
binoculars	망원경	mangwongyong
bird	새	sae
birthday	생일	seng-il

happy birthday!	생일 축하해요!	sengil ch'uk'ahaeyo!
birthday present	생일 선물	sengil sonmul
biscuits	과자	kwaja
bit	조금	chogum
just a bit	조금만	chogumman
to bite	깨물어요	kkemuroyo
bitter (taste)	써요	ssoyo (dic. ssuda)
black (n)	검정	komjong
(adj)	검은	komun
blanket	이불	ibul
to bleed	피나요	p'inayo (dic. p'inada)

English – Korean

English	Korean	Romanization
it won't stop bleeding	계속 피 나요	kesok p'inayo
blind (adj)	장님	changnim
blind (for window)	블라인드	pul-la-in-du
blocked	막힌	mak'in
the sink is blocked	싱크가 막혔어요	sing-k'u-ga mak'yossoyo
blood	피	p'i
blood group	혈액형	hyorek'yong
my blood group is...	내 혈액형은...	nae hyorek'ong-un...
blood pressure	혈압	hyorap
I have high blood pressure	고혈압이에요	kohyorap-iyeyo
blue (n)	파랑	p'arang
(adj)	파란	p'aran
to board (plane)	탑승해요	t'apsung haeyo (dic. t'apsunghada), seungcha
(train)	승차해요	haeyo (dic. sungchahada)
boarding pass	탑승권	t'apsung-kwon
boat	배	pae
boiled rice	밥	pap
bone	뼈	ppyo
book (reading)	책	chek
to book	예약해요	yeyak haeyo (dic. yeyakhada)

English	Korean	Romanization
booking	예약	yeyak
booking office	예약실	yeyakshil
boots	부츠	poo-ch'u
to be born	태어나요	t'eonayo (dic. t'eonada)
I was born in England	나는 영국에서	nanun yongguk-eso
	태어났어요	t'eonassoyo
to borrow	빌려요	pillyoyo (dic. pillida)
can I borrow...?	…빌릴 수 있어요?	…pilli soo issoyo?
botanical gardens	식물원	singmul-won
bottle	병	pyong

English	Korean	Romanization
bottle opener	병따개	pyong ttage
bowl	그릇	kurut
box	상자	sangja
boy	남자아이	namja ai
boyfriend	남자친구	namja chin-gu
bra	브라자	pu-ra-ja
bracelet	팔찌	p'alchi
brake fluid	브레이크 액	pu-re-i-k'u-ek
brake pads	브레이크 패드	pu-re-i-k'u p'e-du
brakes	브레이크	pu-re-i-k'u
branch (bank)	지점	chijom
(company)	지사	chisa
(of tree)	나무가지	namukkaji
brandy	꼬냑	kkonyak

English	Korean			English	Korean	
bread	빵	ppang		bridge (game)	브리지	pu-ri-ji
white bread	흰 빵	hin ppang		(river, road, etc.)	다리	tari
to break	부숴요	puswoyo (dic.		briefcase	서류 가방	sonyu kabang
		dic. pusuda)		to bring (thing)	가지고 와요	kajigo wayo
it has broken	고장났어요	kojang				(dic. kajigo oda)
down		nassoyo		(person)	데리고 와요	terigo wayo
breakfast	아침	ach'im				(dic. terigo oda)
breast (chicken)	가슴살	kasumsal		Britain	영국	yongguk
to breathe	숨을 쉬어요	sumul swi-oyo		British (adj)	영국 (의)	yongguk(e)
		(dic. sumul		(person)	영국 사람	yongguk saram
		swida)		brochure	안내서	anneso
I can't breathe	숨을 못	sumul mot		broken: this is	이거	igo kojang
	쉬겠어요	swigessoyo		broken	고장났어요	nassoyo
bride	신부	shinbu		brothers	형제	hyongje
bridegroom	신랑	shillang				

older brother (own)	형	hyong
brown (n)	갈색	kalsek
(adj)	갈색 (의)	kalsek(e)
Buddha	부처(님)	puch'o(nim)
Buddhism	불교	pulgyo
Buddhist temple	(으) 절	chol
building	건물 / 빌딩	konmul/bil-ding
bulb (light)	전구	chon-gu
bureau de change	환전소	hwanjonso
burn: it's burnt (food)	탔어요	t'assoyo
bus	버스	po-su

business	사업 / 비지니스	saop/ piji-ni-su
business card	명함	myongham
business trip	출장	ch'ulchang
bus station	버스 터미널	po-su t'o-mi-nal
bus stop	버스 정류소	po-su chongnyuso
bus tour: is there a bus tour?	버스 투어가 있어요?	po-su tu-o-ga issoyo?
busy	바빠요	pappayo (dic. pappuda)
are you busy?	바쁘세요?	pappuseyo?

English	Korean	Romanization
the line's busy (phone)	통화중이에요	t'onghwa jungiyeyo.
butcher's	정육점	chong-yukchom
butter	버터	po-t'o
button	단추	tanch'u
to buy	사요 (dic. sada)	sayo (dic. sada)
where can I buy...?	어디서 팔아요?	odiso p'arayo?
by: by bus	택시로	t'ekshi-ro
by car	자동차로	chadongch'a-ro
by plane	기차로	kich'a-ro
by taxi	비행기로	pihenggi-ro
by train	버스로	posu-ro

C

English	Korean	Romanization
cab (taxi)	택시	tekshi
cable car	케이블카	k'e-i-bul-k'a
caddy (golf)	캐디	k'e-di
café	카페	k'a-p'e
cake (western style)	케이크	k'e-i-k'u
cake shop	빵집 / 제과점	ppang-chip/ chegwajom
calculator	계산기	kesan-gi
to call (phone)	...(에) 전화해요	(dic. chonhwa hada)
call (phone call)	전화	chonhwa

English – Korean

long-distance call	장거리 전화	changgori chonhwa
camcorder	비디오 카메라/ 캠코더	pi-di-o-k'a-me-ra/ k'em-k'o-do
camera	카메라	k'a-me-ra
camera bag	카메라 가방	k'a-me-ra kabang
camera shop	카메라 가게	k'a-me-ra kage
camping	캠핑	k'em-p'ing
can we go camping?	캠핑 가는 거 가능해요?	k'em-p'ing kanun go kanung haeyo?
can (n)	깡통	kkang-t'ong

can: can I...?	...가능해요?, ...할 수 있어요?	...kanung haeyo?, ...hal su issoyo?
can (may): may I...?	...해도 돼요?	...haedo tweyo?
can opener	깡통 따개	kkangt'ong tta-ge
Canada	캐나다	k'ae-na-da
Canadian (adj)	캐나다의	k'ae-na-da-e
Canadian (person)	캐나다 사람	k'ae-na-da saram
to cancel	취소해요	ch'wiso haeyo (dic. ch'wiso hada)
I'd like to cancel my booking	예약을 취소하고 싶어요	yeyagul ch'wiso hago sip'oyo

176|177

English – Korean

English	Korean	Romanization
cancellation (of flight/of train)	취소 / 캔슬	ch'wiso/k'en-sul
cancelled	취소됐어요	ch'wiso twessoyo
cancer	암	am
canned	통조림	t'ongjorim
capital (city)	수도	soodo
(money)	자금/자본	chagum/chabon
car	자동차	chadongch'a
car accessories	자동차 부품	chadongch'a poop'um
caravan	카라반	k'a-ra-ban
carburettor	카브레타	k'ya-bu-re-t'a

English	Korean	Romanization
card (business)	명함	myongham
(playing)	트럼프 /	t'u-rom-p'u/
	카드	k'a-du
(greetings)	카드 / 엽서	k'a-du/yopso
card phone	카드용 전화	k'a-du yong chonhwa
careful: be careful!	조심하세요!	chosim haseyo!
I will be very careful	조심하겠어요	chosim hagessoyo
careless	조심성 없는	chosimsong omnun
car hire	렌트카	ren-t'u-k'a
car keys	자동차 열쇠	chadongch'a yolswe

English	Korean	Romanization
car park	주차장	chuch'ajang
carpet	카페트	k'a-p'e-t'u
carriage (train)	객차	kekch'a
carrier bag	가방	kabang
carrot	당근	tanggun
to carry	운반해요	unban haeyo (dic. unban hada)
carsick	차멀미	ch'a-molmi
I get car sick	차멀미 해요	ch'amolmi haeyo
carwash	세차	sech'a
case (suitcase)	여행 가방	yoheng kabang
cash (n)	현금	hyongum

English	Korean	Romanization
we only take	현금만 받아요	hyongum man padayo
cash	현금	hyongum
cash dispenser	현금 인출기	hyongum inchulki
casino	카지노	k'a-ji-no
castle	성	song
cat	고양이	koyang-i
to catch (hold of)	잡다	chabayo (dic. chapta)
to catch a cold	감기 걸렸어요	kamgi kollyossoyo
cathedral	성당	songdang
catholic	천주교	ch'onjugyo
cauliflower	컬리플라워	k'ol-li-p'ul-la-wo
cave	동굴	tonggul

English	Korean		English	Korean	
CD	시디	si-di	certain: *are you certain?*	정말이에요?	chongmariyeyo?
CD player	시디 플레이어	si-di-pul-le-i-o	certainly *(truth)*	확실히	hwakshiri
cemetery	묘지	myoji	certainly! *(I will do that)*	정말로!	chongmallo!
centigrade	섭씨	sopssi	chair	의자	uija
centimetre	센티미터	sen-t'i-mi-t'o	champagne	샴페인	sham-p'e-in
central	중심	chungshim	change *(money)*	잔돈	chandon
central heating	중앙난방	chung-ang nanbang	changing room	탈의실	t'aluishil
centre	중심 / 중앙	chungshim/ chung-ang	charge *(fee)*	요금	yogum
			charge: *is there any charge?*	돈 내야 돼요?	ton neya tweyo?
century	세기	segi	free of charge	무료	mooryo
21st century	이십일 세기	iship ilsegi	to check	체크하다 / 점토하다	ch'e-k'u hada/ komt'o hada
ceramics	도자기	tojagi			
cereal *(breakfast)*	시리얼	si-ri-ol			

English	Korean		English	Korean
can you check this for me?	이거 좀 체크해 주세요?	igo chom ch'ek'u hae chuseyo?	chemist's (shop)	약국	yakkuk
			cheque	수표	soop'yo
to check in:			cherry	앵두 / 체리	engdu/ch'eri
where do I check in?	어디서 체크인 해요?	odiso ch'e-k'u-in haeyo?	cherry blossom	벚꽃	potkkot
			chest (of body)	가슴	kasum
			chewing gum	껌	kkom
check-in desk (hotel)	프론트	p'u-ron-t'u	chicken (bird)	닭	tak
			(meat)	닭고기	takkogi
to check out:			(grilled)	통닭	t'ongdak
when should I check out by?	몇 시까지 체크아웃해야 돼요?	myossi kkaji ch'ek'u-a-ut haeya tweyo?	chickenpox	수두	soodoo
			children	아이들	aidul
			chilli	고추	koch'oo
cheers!	건배!	konbe!	China	중국	chungguk
cheese	치즈	ch'i'ju			
chef	주방장	chupangjang			

English	Korean	Romanization	English	Korean	Romanization
Chinese (adj)	중국 (의)	chungguke	church	교회	kyohwe
(person)	중국사람	chungguk saram	cigar	씨가	si-ga
(language)	중국말	chungguk mal	cigarette	담배	tambe
chips	감자튀김	kamja t'wigim	cigarette lighter	라이타	la-i-t'a
(French fries)	(후렌치 후라이)	(hurenchi hurai)	cinema (place)	영화관	yonghwagwan
chocolate(s)	초콜렛	ch'o-k'o-let	city	도시	toshi
to choose	콜라요	kollayo	city centre	시내 / 도심	shinae/toshim
		(dic. koruda)	claim (n)	반	k'ul-le-im
you choose	대신 콜라	taeshin kola	class (in school)	반	pan
for me	주세요	chuseyo	business class	비지니스 클래스	pijinisu k'ul-la-su
chopsticks	젓가락	chotkarak	economy class	일반석	ilbansok
Christian name	세례명	seremyong	first class	일등석	iltungsok
Christmas	성탄절	songt'anjol	second class	이등석	itungsok
Christmas Eve	성탄전야	songt'an chonya			

English	Korean	Romanization
classical music	고전 음악, 클래식	kojon umak, kraesik
clean (adj)	깨끗해요	kkekkut'eyo
to clean (house)	청소해요	ch'ongso haeyo
cleaner (person)	청소부	ch'ongsobu
clever	똑똑해요	ttokttok'eyo
climate	기후	kihoo
climbing (mountains)	등산	tungsan
climbing boots	등산화	tungsanhwa
clinic	병원	pyongwon
clock	시계	shige
to close	닫아요 (닫다)	tadayo (dic. tatta)

English	Korean	Romanization
when do you close?	몇 시에 닫아요?	myossi-e tadayo?
closed (shops)	닫았어요, 휴업	tachyeossoyo, hyu-op
cloth	헝겊	honggop
clothes	옷 / 의류	ot/uiryu
cloudy	흐려요	hunyoyo
club	(dic. hurida)	
club	클럽	k'ul-lop
clutch (car)	클러치	k'ul-lo-ch'i
coach (bus)	대행버스	taehyong po-su
coach (of train)	객자	kekch'a
coach station	버스 터미널	po-su t'o-mi-nal
coast	해변	hebyon
coat	외투	wet'oo

English – Korean

English	Korean	Romanization
Coca Cola®	코카콜라	k'o-k'a-k'ol-la
coffee	커피	k'o-p'i
black coffee	블랙커피	pul-lek-k'o-p'i
decaffeinated coffee	디카페인 커피	ti-k'a-p'e-in- k'o-p'i
white coffee	밀크커피	mil-k'u-k'o-p'i
cappuccino	카푸치노	k'a-p'u-ch'i-no
cognac	꼬냑	kko-nyak
coin	코인 / 동전	k'o-in/tongjon
cold: it's cold (room)	추위요 (춥다)	ch'uwoyo (dic. ch'upta)
cold	추워요 (춥다)	kamgi
I have a cold	감기 걸렸어요	kamgi kollyossoyo

English	Korean	Romanization
colleague	동료	tongnyo
college (university)	대학	taehak
(junior college)	전문 대학	chonmun taehak
colour	색 / 색깔	sek/sekkal
colour film (for camera)	컬러 필름	k'al-la-p'il-lim
comb	빗	pit
to come	와요 (오다)	wayo (dic. oda)
when can you come?	언제 올 수 있어요?	onje olsoo issoyo?
come in!	들어 오세요!	turo oseyo!
comedy	코메디	k'o-me-di

comfortable	편안해요 (편안하다)	p'yonan haeyo (dic. p'yonan hada)
this is very comfortable	아주 편안해요	aju p'yonan haeyo
comics (publications)	만화	manhwa
commercial (on TV)	광고	kwanggo
common (usual)	보통	pot'ong
compact disc	콤팩트 디스크	k'om-p'ek-t'u-di-su-k'u
company (firm)	회사	hwesa
company director	사장	sajang

compartment (train)	객실	kekshil
competitive price	저렴한 가격	churyomhan kagyok
complaint	불평/ 컴플레인	pulp'yong/ k'om-p'ul-le-in
I have a complaint	컴플레인 있어요	k'om-p'ul-le-in issoyo
to complete	끝내요 (끝내다)	kkunneyo (dic. kkunneda)
complicated	복잡해요 (복잡하다)	pokchap'eyo (dic. pokchap'ada)

it's very complicated	아주 복잡해요	aju pokchap'eyo	conditioner (hair)	린스	lin-su
compulsory: is it compulsory?	꼭 해야 돼요?	kkok heya tweyo?	condom	콘돔	k'on-dom
computer	컴퓨터	k'ŏm-p'yu-t'o	conductor (music)	지휘자	chihwija
computer game	컴퓨터 게임	k'ŏm-p'yu-t'o ge-im	conference	회의	hwe-i
computer programmer	컴퓨터 프로그래머	k'ŏm-p'yu-t'o p'u-ro-gu-re-mo	conference centre	회의장	hwe-i-jang
concert	연주회	yonjuhwe	to confirm: *do I need to confirm?*	확인해야 돼요?	hwagin heya tweyo?
concert hall	연주회장	yonjuhwejang	*I want to confirm my booking*	예약을 확인하고 싶어요.	yeyag-ul hwagin hago sip'oyo.
concussion (medical)	뇌진탕, 진동	noejintang, chindong			

congratu-lations	축하해요 (축하하다)	ch'uk'a haeyo (dic. ch'uk'a hada)	contact lenses	콘택트 렌즈	k'on-t'ek-t'u len-ju
to connect: I'm trying to connect you	연결하고 있어요	yongyolp'yon issoyo	continent	대륙	taeryuk
			contraceptive (n)	피임약	p'iimnyak
connection (train, plane, etc.)	연결편	yongyolp'yon	controls (car)	콘트롤	k'on-t'u-rol
			convenient	편리해 요	p'yolli haeyo
connection (electronic)	연결선	yongyolson	cook (n)	요 리사	yorisa
constipated: I'm constipated	변비예요	pyonbi yyeyo	to cook	요 리해 요 (dic. yori hada)	yori haeyo
consul	영사	yongsa	cooker	쿠커	k'u-k'o
consulate	영사관	yongsagwan	copy (n)	복사	poksa
contact lens cleaner	콘택트 렌즈 세 척 액	k'on-t'ek-t'u len-ju sech'ogek	can I make a copy?	복사 가능해 요 ?	poksa kanung haeyo?
			corkscrew	병따개	pyong ttage

corn	옥수수	oksoosoo	counter (in shop, etc.)	계산대	kesande
corner	코너 / 골목	k'o-no/kolmok	country (not town)	시골	shigol
correct: is it correct?	맞아요?	majayo?	(state)	나라	nara
corridor	복도	pokto	couple (people)	커플	k'o-p'ul
cost (n)	비용	piyong	courier	속달	soktal
to cost: how much does it cost?	비용이 얼마예요?	piyong-i piyong-i-olma yeyo?	I want to send this by courier	속달로 보내고 싶어요	soktal-lo ponego sip oyo
cotton	면 / 솜	myon/som	course (study)	코스	k'o-su
cotton wool	면	myon	(meal)	코스 메뉴	k'o-su menyu
cough (n)	기침	kich'im	of course	물론	mullon
to count	계산해요 (계산하다)	kesan haeyo (dic. kesan hada)	court (law)	법정	popchong
			(tennis)	코트	k'o-t'u

crab	게	ke
crafts	공예	kong-ye
cream	크림	k'u-rim
credit	신용	shinyong
credit card	신용카드	shinyong k'a-du
crisps	감자 튀김	kamja t'wigim
cross (n)	사거리 / 십자가	sagori/ shipchaga
crossing (ferry): when is the next crossing?	다음 페리는 언제예요?	taum p'e-ri-nun onje yeyo?
crossroads	십자로	shipcharo
crowd	사람들	saramdul
crown (on tooth)	크라운, 치관	k'u-ra-un, chikwan

cruise (n)	크루즈, 배 여행	kuruju, pae yoheng
to cry (weep)	울어요 (울다)	ooroyo (dic. oolda)
cucumber	오이	o-i
cup	컵	k'op
cupboard	선반	sonban
cure (healing, remedy)	치료 (법)	ch'inyo
current (electricity)	전류	chollyu
curtains	카텐	k'o-t'en
cushion	구선	k'u-shyon
customs	세관	segwan

English	Korean	Romanization
customs declaration	세관 신고	segwan shin-go
cut (n)	잔아요	k'o-t'u
to cut	잔아요 (잔다)	kkakkayo (dic. kkakta)
cutlery	수저	soojo
cybercafé	인터넷 카페	in-t'o-net k'a-p'e
cycling	싸이클링	sa-i-k'ul-ling
D		
daily (each day)	매일	meil
dance (n)	춤	ch'um
to dance	춤춰요	ch'um ch'woyo
dangerous	위험해요	wihom haeyo

English	Korean	Romanization
dark (colour)	어두운	odu-un
date (day of month)	날짜	nalcha
(formal appointment)	데이트	te-i-t'u
date of birth	생일	seng-il
daughter	딸	ttal
day	날	nal
per day	하루에	haru-e
every day	매일	meil
deaf	귀머거리	kwimogori
dear (expensive)	비싼	pissan
decaffeinated	카페인 없는	k'a-p'e-in omnun
December	십이월	shibiwol
deep	깊은	kip'un

degree (temperature)	도	to	도
university	하위		hagwi
delay: *how long is the delay?*	얼마나 지연돼요?		olmana chiyon tweyo?
to be delayed (plane, train, etc.)	지연돼요		chiyon tweyo
dentist	치과의사		ch'ikwa uisa
dentures	의치		uich'i
deodorant	데오도란트, 방취제		deodorant, panchuije
department store	백화점		pek wajom
departure	출발		ch'ulbal

departure lounge	출발 라운지	ch'ulbal la-un-ji
deposit (to pay)	보증금	pojunggum
dessert	디저트 / 후식	ti-jo-t'u/hooshik
destination	목적지	mokchokchi
detergent	세제	seje
diabetic	당뇨병	tangnyopyong
to dial	전화해요	chohwa haeyo
diarrhoea	설사	solsa
diary	일기	ilgi
dictionary	사전	sajon
diet	다이어트	ta-i-o-t'u
different	다른	tarun
digital camera	디지털	tiji-t'ol
	카메라	k'a-me-ra

English – Korean

dining room	식당	shiktang	disk	디스크	ti-su-k'u
dinner	저녁 식사/	chonyok shiksa/	disposable	일회용	ilhweyong
	석식	sokshik	district	지역	chiyok
direct (train, etc.)	직행	chik'eng	divorce (n)	이혼	ihon
			divorced	이혼한	ihonhan
direction	방향	panghyang	dizzy: to feel	어지러워요	ojirowoyo
directory	주소록	chusorok	dizzy	(어지럽다)	(dic. ojiropta)
dirty	더러워요	torowoyo	to do	해요 (하다)	haeyo (dic. hada)
	(더럽다)	(dic. toropta)	doctor	의사	uisa
disabled	장애자	chang-eja	document	서류	soryu
disco	디스코	ti-su-k'o	dog	개	kae
discount	할인/	harin/ti-su-	dollar	달러	tal-lo
	디스가운트	k'a-un-t'u	door	문	moon
dish	접시	chopshi	double (quantity)	두 배 / 곱빼기	tu pe/koppegi
disinfectant	소독약	sodongnyak			

English	Korean	Romanization
double bed	더블 베드	to-bul-be-du
double room	더블룸/ 이인용 방	to-bul rum/ iinyong pang
download	다운로드	ta-un-lo-du
dress (n)	드레스	tu-re-su
dressing (medical)	붕대	pungde
(salad)	드레싱	tu-re-ssing
drink	음료수	umnyosoo
to drink	마셔요 (마시다)	mashyoyo (dic. mashida)
to drive	운전해요 (운전하다)	unjon haeyo (dic. unjon hada)
driver (of car)	운전수	unjonsu

English	Korean	Romanization
driving licence	운전 면허	unjon
		myonho-chung
drug (medical)	약	yak
to dry	말려요 (말리다)	mallyoyo (dic. mallida)
(clothes, etc.)	세탁소	set'akso
dry-cleaner's	오리	ori
duck	면세	myonse
duty-free	이불	ibool
duvet		
E		
ear	귀	kwi
earache	귀가 아파요	kwi-ga ap'ayo
early	일찍	ilchik
earplugs	귀마개	kwi mage

English – Korean

English	Korean	
earrings	귀걸이	kwigori
earthquake	지진	chijin
east	동 (쪽)	tong(chok)
Easter	부활절	puhwalchol
to eat	먹어요 (먹다)	mogoyo (dic. mokta)
eel	장어	chang-o
egg	달걀	talgyal
fried egg	달걀 후라이	talgyal hu-ra-i
hard-boiled egg	삶은 달걀	salmun talgyal
egg scrambled	스크램블드 에그	su-k-u-rem-bul-du e-gu
eggs		
electrician	전기공	chon-gigong
electricity	전기	chon-gi

English	Korean	
electric razor	전기 면도기	chon-gi myondogi
elevator	엘리베이터, 승강기	el-li-be-i-t'o, sungganggi
e-mail	전자우편, 이메일	chonja, oop'yon/i-meil
embassy	대사관	tesagwan
emergency	비상	pisang
emergency exit	비상구	pisanggu
emperor	황제	hwangje
empty	빈	pin

engaged			entrance	입구	ipku
(couple)	약혼해요 (약혼하다)	yak'on haeyo (dic. yak'on hada)	entrance fee	입장료	ipchangnyo
(phone)	통화중	t'onghwajung	envelope	봉투	pongt'u
(toilet)	사용중	sayong jung	epileptic	간질	kanjil
England	영국	yongguk	epileptic fit	간질 발작	kanjil palchak
English (adj)	영국 (의)	yongguk-e	equipment	설비	solbi
(person)	영국 사람	yongguk saram	escalator	에스컬레이터	e-su-k'ol-le-i-t'o
(language)	영어	yong-o	euro	유로	yu-ro
enough: *that's enough* (food, etc.)	됐어요	twessoyo	Europe	유럽	yurop
enquiry desk	안내 창구	anne ch'anggu	evening	저녁	chonyok
to enter (a place)	들어가요 (들어가다)	turogayo (dic. turogada)	in the evening	저녁에	chonyoge
			evening meal	저녁식사 / 석식	chonyok shiksa / sokshik
			example: *for example*	예를 들면	yerul tulmyon

English – Korean

English	Korean	Romanization
excellent	훌륭해요	hullyung haeyo
excess	초과 화물	ch'ogwa
baggage	화물	hwamul
exchange rate	환율	hwannyul
excursion	소풍	sop'ung
excuse me!	실례합니다!	sillyehamnida!
exhibition	전시회	chonshihwe
exit	출구	ch'ulgu
expensive	비싸요	pissayo
exports	수출품	sooch'ulp'um
express train	고속열차	kosok yolch'a
extension (electrical)	연결선	yongolson
(phone)	교환	kyohwan
eye	눈	noon

English	Korean	Romanization
eye drops	안약	anyak
F		
fabric	옷감	otkam
factory	공장	kongjang
to faint	기절해요	kijol haeyo
false teeth	틀니 / 의치	t'ulni/uich'i
family	가족	kajok
fan (hand-held)	부채	puch'e
(electric)	선풍기	sonp'unggi
far	멀어요	moroyo
fare (bus, etc.)	요금	yogum
Far East	극동	kuktong
farm	농장	nongjang
fast	빨라요	ppallayo

fat (person)	뚱뚱해요	ttungttung haeyo	
father	아버지	aboji	
faulty (machine, etc.)	결함 있어요	kyolham issoyo	
fax	팩스	p'ek-su	
to fax	팩스 보내요	p'ek-su poneyo	
fax number	팩스 번호	p'ek-su ponho	
February	이월	i-wol	
fee	요금	yogum	
female (adj)	여자 (의)	yoja(e)	
ferry	페리	p'e-ri	
festival	축제	ch'ukche	
few: a few	조금	chogum	
fiancé(e)	약혼자	yak'onja	

file (computer, document)	파일	p'a-il	
to fill (up)	채워요	ch'ewoyo	
fill it up!	꽉 채우세요!	kwak ch'euseyo!	
filling (tooth)	봉	pong	
film (for camera)	필름	p'il-lim	
film (cinema)	영화	yonghwa	
to find	찾아요	ch'ajayo	
I can't find...	(찾다)	(dic. ch'atta)	
	...못	...mot	
fine (penalty)	벌금	polgum	
finger	손가락	sonkarak	
fire: house fire	불 / 화재	pool/hwaje	
camp fire	캠프 화이어	k'em-p'u-p'a-i-o	

English	Korean		English	Korean	
fire alarm	화재 경보기	hwajae kyongbogi	fish (n)	생선	sengson
fire brigade	소방대	sobangdae	to fit: it doesn't fit	안 맞아요	an majayo
fire escape	비상출구	pisang ch'ulgu	fitting room	탈의실	t'aluishil
fire extinguisher	소화기	sohwagi	to fix: can you fix it?	고쳐 주세요?	koch'yo chuseyo?
fireworks	불꽃놀이	pulkkonnori	flat (apartment)	아파트	ap'a-t'u
firm (company)	회사	hwesa	flat tyre	배터리가 앉어요	paettu-ri-ga opssoyo
first	최초 / 처음	ch'wech'o / ch'oum	flavour	평크	p'ong-k'u
first aid	응급치료	unggup ch'iryo	floor (of building)	맛	mat
first aid kit	구급약세트	kugumnyak se-t'u	first floor	-층	-ch'ung
first class	일등석	iltungsok	second floor	일층	iilch'ung
first floor (above ground floor)	이층	i-ch'ung	flower	이층	i-ch'ung
first name	이름	irum		꽃	kkot

English	Korean (Hangul)	Korean (Romanized)
flu	독감	tokkam
fly (insect)	파리	p'ari
to fly	날아요	narayo
	(날다)	(dic. nalda)
food	음식	umshik
food poisoning	식중독	shikchungdok
foot	다리	tari
football (soccer)	축구	ch'ukku
for (in exchange for)	…대신	…teshin
foreign	외국	weguk
forest	숲	soop
fork (cutlery)	포크	p'o-k'u
fortnight	이주간	ijugan
fountain	분수	punsoo

English	Korean (Hangul)	Korean (Romanized)
foyer	로비	lo-bi
fracture (of bone)	골절	kolchol
fragrance	향기	hyanggi
frame (picture)	액자	ekcha
free	비어 있는	pio innun
(not occupied)	무료	mooyo
(costing nothing)	자유	chayu
(not constrained)	신선한	shinsonhan
fresh (food)	금요일	kumyoil
Friday	냉장고	nengjanggo
fridge	튀긴 음식	t'wigin umshik
fried food	친구	ch'in-gu
friend	과일	kwa-il
fruit		

fruit juice	과일 쥬스	kwaiil chu-su	
fuel	연료	yollyo	
full	꽉	kkwak	
full board	식사 제공	shiksa chegong	
funny (amusing)	재미있는	chemi-innun	
(strange)	웃기는	ookkinun	
fuse	퓨즈	p'yu-ju	
fuse box	두꺼비집 /	tukkobijip/	
	퓨즈박스	p'yu-ju-bak-su	

garlic	마늘	manul	
gate	문	moon	
(airport)	게이트	ke-i-t'u	
gay (bright)	명랑한	myongnanghan	
(homosexual)	게이 /	ke-i/tongsong	
	동성연애자	yoneja	
gears	기어	ki-o	
generous	관대한	kwandehan	
gentleman	신사	shinsa	
gents (toilet)	남자 화장실	namja	
		hwajangshil	

G

gallery	갤러리	kel-lo-ri	
game	게임	ke-im	
garage	차고	ch'ago	
garden	정원	chongwon	

English	Korean	
to get (obtain)	갖고 있어요 (갖고 있다)	katko issoyo (dic. katko itta)
to fetch thing)	갖고 와요	katko wayo
(to fetch person, animal)	데려 와요	teryo wayo
to get in (car)	타요 (타다)	t'ayo (dic. t'ada)
to get off	내려요	naeryoyo
(bus, etc.)	(내리다)	(dic. naerida)
gift	선물	sonmul
gift shop	선물 가게	sonmul kage
ginger	생강	senggang
girl	소녀	sonyo
girlfriend	여자친구	yoja chin-gu
to give	줘요 (주다)	chwoyo (dic. chuda)

English	Korean	
to give back	돌려 줘요	tollyo chwoyo
glass	유리/잔	yuri/chan
glasses (spectacles)	안경	angyong
gloves	장갑	changgap
glue	풀	p'ool
to go	가요 (가다)	kayo (dic. kada)
to go back	돌아가요	toragayo
to go in	들어가요	turogayo
to go out	나가요	nagayo
	(나가다)	(dic. ngada)
gold	금	kum
golf	골프	kol-p'u
golf ball	골프 공	kol-p'u kong
golf club	골프 클럽	kol-p'u k'ul-lop

English – Korean

golf course	골프 코스	kol-p'u k'o-su	
good	좋아요	choayo	
good *afternoon*	안녕하세요	annyong haseyo	
goodbye	안녕히 가세요	annyonghi kaseyo	
good evening	안녕하세요	annyong haseyo	
good morning	안녕하세요	annyong haseyo	
goodnight	안녕히 주무세요	annyonghi chumuseyo	
granddaughter	손녀 (딸)	sonnyo(ttal)	
grandfather	할아버지	haraboji	
grandmother	할머니	halmoni	
grandson	손자	sonja	
grapefruit	자몽	chamong	

grapes	포도	p'odo	
great (large),	큰	k'un	
green	초록 (색)	ch'orok(sek)	
greengrocer	야채 가게	yach'e kage	
grey	회색	hwesek	
grilled	군 / 구운	kun/ku-un	
ground floor	일층	ilch'ung	
group (people)	그룹	ku-roop	
guarantee (n)	보증	pojung	
guard (on train)	차장	ch'ajang	
guest (to house)	손님	sonnim	
guesthouse	게스트 하우스	ke-su-t'u-ha-u-su	
guide (n)	가이드 / 안내	ka-i-du/anne	

English	Korean	Romanization
to guide	가이드하다 / 안내하다	kaidu haeyo / anne haeyo
guidebook	가이드북	ka-i-du-book
guided tour	가이드 투어	ka-i-du-t'u-o

H

English	Korean	Romanization
hair	머리 (털)	mon(t'ol)
hairbrush	머리빗	moribit
haircut	이발 / 헤어컷	ibal / he-o-k'ot
hairdresser's		
(for men)	이발소	ibalso
(for women)	미장원	mijangwon
hairdryer	헤어 드라이어	he-o-du-ra-i-o
hairspray	헤어 스프레이	he-o-su-p'u-re-i
half: *half a bottle of...*	반 / 반 병	pan / panbyong
half-price (for concerts, etc.)	반값 / 반액	pan kap / panek
hall	홀	hol
ham	햄	haem
hand luggage	핸드러기지 / 손가방	hen-du-lo-gi-ji / songbang
handbag	핸드백	hen-du-bek
handkerchief	손수건	sonsoogon
handmade	수제품	soojep'um
to happen	발생하다	palseng haeyo

English – Korean

English	Korean	Romanization
what happened?	무슨 일이에요?	musun ireyo?
hard (firm)	딱딱한 (딱딱하다)	ttakttak'eyo (dic. ttakttak'ada)
(difficult)	어려운 (어렵다)	oryowo (dic. oryopta)
hayfever	해이 피버 / 화분증	he-i-p'i-bo/ hwabunjung
head	머리	mori
head office	본사 / 본점	ponsa/ponjom
headache	두통	tut'ong
headlights	전조등	chonjodung
headphones	헤드폰	he-du-p'on
hearing aid	보청기	poch'onggi

English	Korean	Romanization
heart (emotional)	마음	maum
(organ)	심장	simjang
heart attack	심장마비	simjang mabi
to heat up (food)	데우다 /	deuda/
	덥히다	duphida
heater	히터	hi-t'o
heavy (weight)	무거운 (무겁다)	mogowoyo (dic. mugopta)
hello (on phone)	안녕하세요?	annyonghaseyo?
	여보세요	yoboseyo
to help	도와주다	towa juwoyo
help!	도와주세요!	towa juseyo!
here	여기	yogi
high	높아요	nop'ayo

English	Korean	Romanization
high blood pressure	고혈압	kohyorap
hill-walking	하이킹	haiking
to hire	빌려요	pilljoyo
can I hire...?	(빌리다) ...렌트 가능해요?	(dic. pillida) ...ren-t'u kanung haeyo?
hobby	취미	ch'wimi
holiday	휴가/휴일	hyuga/hyuil
on holiday	휴가중	hyugajung
national holiday	공휴일	konghyuil
homesick	향수병	hyangsoopyong
(to be)	(걸렸어요)	kollyossoyo
honey	꿀	kkool
honeymoon	신혼 여행	shinhon yoheng
horse	말	mal
horseradish	겨자	kyoja
hospital	병원	pyongwon
host (at dinner, etc.)	호스트	ho-su-t'u
hostel	유스호스텔	yu-su-ho-su-t'el
hot	뜨거운/더운 (뜨겁다)	ttugowoyo (dic. ttugopta)
hotel	호텔	ho-t'el
Korean hotel (traditional)	여관	yogwan
(B&B)	민박	minbak
hour	시간	shigan
one hour	한 시간	han shigan

English – Korean

two hours	두 시간	tu shigan
house	집	chip
house wine	하우스 와인	house wain
housewife	(가정) 주부	(kajong) chubu
how: how much/many?	얼마나?	olmana?
hungry: I'm hungry	배가 고파요	pega kop'ayo
hurry: I'm in a hurry	급해요	kup'eyo
to hurt: (my back) hurts	(등이) 아파요	(tung-i) ap'ayo
husband	남편	namp'yon

I

– (polite)	나	na
–	저	cho
ice	얼음	orum
ice-cream	아이스크림	ai-su-k'u-rim
identity card	신분증	shinbunjung
ignition key	자동차 열쇠	chadongch'a yolswe
ill: ...is ill	아파요	ap'ayo
illegal	불법 (의)	pulbop(e)
immediately	곧/즉시	kot/chukshi
important	중요해요	chungyo haeyo
imports	수입품	sooipp'um
indigestion	소화불량	sohwapoollyang
inflammation	연소	yonso

information	정보	chongbo	instant coffee	인스턴트 커피	insu-t'on-t'u k'o-p'i
information office	안내소	anneso	instructions (for use)	사용 설명서	sayong solmyongso
inhaler	(인공) 호흡기	(ingong) hohupki	insulin	인슐린	in-syul-lin
injection	주사	chusa	insurance	보험	pohom
to be injured	다쳤어요 (다치다)	tach'yossoyo (dic. tach'ida)	insurance certificate	보험 증서	pohom chungso
inquiry desk	안내소	anneso	international	국제 적	kukchejok
insect	곤충	konch'ung	Internet	인터넷	in-t'o-net
insect repellent	방충제	pangch'ungje	Internet café	인터넷 카페	in-t'o-net k'a-p'e
inside...	...안에	...ane	interpreter (theatre)	통역사	t'ong-yoksa
inside the car	자동차 안에	chadongch'a ane	interval	휴식 (시간)	hyushik-shigan

English – Korean

206 | 207

English – Korean

to introduce (a person)	소개해요	soge haeyo
invitation	좀대	ch'ode
to invite	좀대해요	ch'ode haeyo
invoice	청구서	ch'ongguso
Ireland	아일랜드 / 에이레	a-il-len-du/ e-i-re
Irish (adj)	아일랜드	a-il-len-du
(person)	아일랜드 사람	a-il-len-du saram
iron (for clothes)	다림질	tarimjil
(metal)	다리미	tarimi
ironmonger's	철물점	ch'olmuljom
island	섬	som
itemized bill	명세서	myongseso

J

jacket	자킷	chak'et
jam (food)	쨈	chem
traffic jam	교통 체증	kyot'ong ch'ejung
January	일월	ilwol
Japan	일본	ilbon
jeweller's	보석상	posoksang
jewellery	보석	posok
job	직업 / 일	chigop/il
to jog	조깅해요	choging haeyo
journey	여행	yoheng
juice (fruit) (of something)	쥬스	chyu-su
	액	aek
July	칠월	ch'irwol

junction (roads)	교차로	kyoch'aro
June	유월	yuwol
just: *just two*	둘만	tul man
I've just	방금	panggum
arrived	도착했어요	toch'ak'essoyo

K

key (for lock)	열쇠	yolswe
kidneys (food)	콩팥	k'ongp'at
kilo	킬로	k'illo
kilometre	킬로미터	k'illomit'o
kind (n)	종류	chongnyu
(adj)	친절해요	ch'injol haeyo
kitchen	부엌	puok
knickers	내복/속옷	naebok/sokot

knife	칼	k'al
to knock	(자동차가)	(cadongch'aga)
down (car)	고장났어요	kojangnassoyo
knot	매듭	medup
to know (facts)	알아요	arayo
	(알다)	(dic. alda)
I don't know	저는 서울을	chonun soul-ul
Seoul	몰라요	mollayo
Korea	한국	han-guk
Korean	한국말	han-gungmal
(language)		
(adj)	한국 (의)	han-guk(e)
(person)	한국 사람	han-guk saram

208 | 209

English – Korean

L

English	Korean	
label	라벨 / 상표	rabel/sangp'yo
lace	레이스	re~i-su
shoe lace	구두끈	kudu-kkun
ladies (toilet)	여자 화장실	yoja hwajang-shil
lake	호수	ho-soo
land (n)	토지	t'o-ji
language	말 / 언어	mal/on-o
large	큰	k'un
late	늦은 / 지연된	nujun/chiyon-twen
The train is late	기차가 지연됐어요	kich'a-ga chiyon-twe-ssoyo
launderette	세탁소	set'ak-so

English	Korean	
laundry service	세탁 서비스	set'ak so-bi-su
lavatory	화장실	hwachangshil
lawyer	변호사	pyon-ho-sa
leader (of group)	리더/지도자	li-do/chidoja
leaflet	안내서	an-ne-so
leak (n) (of gas, liquid)	누출	nuch'ul
to learn	배워요	pewoyo (dic. pe-oo-ta)
leather	가죽	kajuk
to leave	떠나요 / 줄여받게요	tto-nayo/ch'ulbalhaeyo
(leave behind)	남겨놓아요	namgyo no-ayo
left	왼쪽	wen-cchok
on/to the left	왼쪽에	wen-cchoge

English	Korean	Romanization
left luggage (office)	수하물 보관소	soo-hamul po-gwanso
leg	다리	tari
lens	렌즈	ren-ju
letter (mail)	편지	p'yonji
letterbox	편지함	p'yonji-ham
lettuce	상추	sang-ch'oo
library	도서관	toso-gwan
licence	면허증	myon-ho-jung
to lie down	누워 있어요 (누워 있다)	nuwo issoyo (dic. nuwo itta)
life jacket	라이프재킷	ra-i-p'u-che-k'it
lifebelt	안전 벨트	anjon pel-t'u
lifeboat	구명보트	kumyong po-t'u
lifeguard	구조원	kujowon
lift (elevator)	엘리베이터	el-li-be-i-t'o
light bulb	전구	chon-gu
lighter	라이터	ra-i-t'o
do you have a lighter?	라이터 있어요?	ra-i-t'o issoyo?
to like	좋아해요	choa haeyo
I like coffee	커피 좋아해요	k'o-p'i choa haeyo
like this	이렇게	irok'e
line (railway)	선	son
(drawn)	줄	chul
list	표 / 리스트 ...(을/를)	p'yo/li-su-t'u ...ul turoyo
to listen to...	들을요 (듣다)	(dic. tut-ta)

English – Korean

litre	리터	ri-t'o
a little	조금	chogum
to live (in a place)	살아요 (살다)	sarayo (dic. sal-ta)
I live in London	런던에 살아요	ron-don-e sarayo
to be alive	살아 있어요 (살아 있다)	sara issoyo (dic. sara it-ta)
he is alive	그 사람은 살아있어요	ku saram-un sara issoyo
liver	간	kan
living room	거실	koshil
lobster	바닷가게	pada kaje
local	지방	chibang

lock (on door, box)	자물쇠	cha-mul-swe
to lock	잠가요 (잠그다)	cham-gayo (dic. cham-gu-ta)
locker	라커	la-k'o
long	오래	o-rae
for a long time	오래동안	o-rae-tong-an
to look for	찾아요 (찾다)	ch'a-jayo (dic. ch'at-ta)
loose (not fastened)	풀어졌어요 (풀어지다)	p'uro-jyossoyo (dic. puro-jida)
to lose	잃어버려요 (잃어버리다)	iro-boryossoyo (dic. iro-borida)

English	Korean	
I've lost...	... (을) 잃어버렸어요	iroboryossoyo
	...ul 잃어버린	iro-borin
lost (object)	분실물	punshil-mul
lost-property office	보관소	po-gwan-so
lotion	로션	lo-shyon
loud	시끄러운	shi-kku-ro-un
love (n)	사랑	sa-lang
I love swimming	수영을 아주 좋아해요	soo-yong-ul aju choa haeyo
luggage	짐 / 수하물	chim/ soo-ha-mul
luggage allowance	수하물 한도	soo-ha-mul hando
lunch	점심	chom-shim
luxury	고급	kogup

M

English	Korean	
machine	기계	ki-ge
magazine	잡지	chap-chi
mail (n)	우편	oo-p'yon
by mail	우편으로	oo-p'yon-uro
to make	만들어요 (만들다)	manduroyo (dic. mandul-ta)
make-up	화장	hwajang
man (general)	사람	saram
(male)	남자	namja
manager	책임자 / 매니저	che-gim-ja/ me-ni-jo
many	많이	man(h)i

English - Korean

map	지도	chido	to matter	중요해요 chung-yo haeyo
marathon	마라톤	ma-ra-t'on		(중요하다) (dic. chung-yo hada)
March	삼월	sam-wol		
market	시장	shijang	it doesn't matter	괜찮아요 kwen-ch'a-nayo
marmalade	마마베이드	ma-ma-re-i-du		
to marry	결혼해요	kyol-hon-haeyo	mattress	매트리스 me-t'u-ri-su
	(결혼하다)	(dic. kyol-hon	May	오월 o-wol
		hada)	meal	식사 shik-sa
martial arts	무술	moo-sool	to mean	의미해요 ui-mihaeyo
mask	가면, 마스크	kamyon/		(의미하다) (dic. ui-mi hada)
		ma-su-k'u	what does	이게 무슨 ige musun
mass (in church)	미사	misa	this mean?	의미예요? uimi-yeyo?
match (game)	경기	kyong-gi	meat	고기 kogi
matches	성냥	song-nyang	mechanic	기술자 kisul-cha

English – Korean

medical insurance	의료보험	ui-ryo pohom	
medicine	약	yak	
medieval	중세	chung-se	
to meet	만나요 (만나다)	mannayo (dic. mannada)	
let's meet again	또 만나요	tto mannayo	
meeting	미팅 / 회의	mit'ing/hwe-i	
member (of club, etc.)	회원	hwe-won	
menu	메뉴	me-nyu	
message	메세지	me-se-ji	
metre	미터	mit'o	
microwave	전자렌지	chonja ren-ji	

midday	정오	chong-o	
at midday	정오에	chong-o-e	
middle-aged	중년	chung-nyon	
midnight	한밤중	hanbam-chung	
migraine	편두통	p'yon-du-t'ong	
milk	우유	oo-yu	
semi-skimmed	저지방 우유	cho-jibang oo-yu	
soya milk	두유	too-yu	
millimetre	밀리미터	mil-li-mit'o	
million	백만	peng-man	
mineral water	생수	seng-soo	
minibar	미니 바	mini ba	
minute	분	pun	
one minute	일분	il-bun	

English – Korean

English	Korean	Romanization
two minutes	이 분	i-bun
mirror	거울	ko-ool
to miss (train, etc.)	놓쳐요 (놓치다)	noch'o-yo (dic. noch'ida)
missing (person)	행방불명	hengbang pulmyong
mistake (n)	실수	shil-soo
mobile phone	휴대전화	hyude chonhwa
modem	모뎀	mo-dem
monastery	수도원	soo-do-won
Monday	월요일	wor-ryo-il
money	돈	ton
I have no money	돈이 없어요	ton-i opssoyo
month	월	wol

English	Korean	Romanization
moon	달	tal
more	더	to
more wine	와인 더	wa-in to
please	주세요	chuseyo
no more, thank you	됐어요	twe-ssoyo
morning	아침	ach'im
in the morning	오전에	ojon-e
this morning	오늘 아침	onul ach'im
mosquito	모기	mogi
mother	어머니	omoni
motorway	고속도로	kosok toro
mountain	산	san

mountain bike	마운틴 바이크	ma-un-t'in ba-i-k'u
mouse (animal)	쥐	chwi
(computer)	마우스	ma-u-su
mouth	입	ip
Mr...	...씨/ ...선생님	...ssi/ ...-sonseng-nim
Mrs...	...씨/...부인	...ssi/ ...-puin
Ms...	...씨	...-ssi
much	많이	mani
There's too much	너무 많아요	nomu manayo
museum	박물관	pangmul-gwan
mushroom	버섯	po-sot
music	음악	umak

mussel	홍합	hong-hap
N		
nail (finger)	손톱	son-t'op
(metal)	못	mot
name	이름	irum
What's your name?	이름이 뭐예요?	irum-i mwo-yeyo?
nappy	기저귀	ki-jo-gwi
narrow	좁은	chobun
nationality	국적	kuk-chok
nausea	구역질 / 멀미	ku-yok-chil/ molmi
near	가까운	kakkaun
necessary	필요한	p'inyo-han

English – Korean

neck	목	·mok	New Zealander (person)	뉴질렌드 사람
necklace	목걸이	mok-kori	news	뉴스
to need	필요해요	p'iryo haeyo	newspaper	신문
	(필요하다)	(dic. p'iryo hada)	next	다음
I need…	…가	…ga p'iryo	next week	다음 주
	필요해요	haeyo	next year	내년
needle	바늘	panul	the next train	다음 기차
neighbour	이웃	i-oot	night	밤
nephew	조카	cho-k'a	at night	밤에
never	절대	chol-tte	last night	어제 밤
I never drink wine	절대 와인 안 마셔요	chol-tte wa-in an masyoyo	tomorrow night	내일 밤
new	새	sae	nightclub	나이트 클럽
New Year	새해	se-he		
New Zealand	뉴질렌드	nyu-jil-len-du		

nyu-jil-len-du saram	
nyu-su	
shim-mun	
taum	
taum-chu	
ne-nyen	
taum kich'a	
pam	
pam-e	
oje pam	
ne-il pam	
na-i-t'u k'ul-lop	

English	Korean	Romanization
nightdress	잠옷	cham-ot
no	아니오	anio
no, thank you	괜찮아요	kwen-ch'a-nayo
noisy	시끄러운	shi-kku-ro-un
non-alcoholic	비알코올성	bialkolsung
non-smoking	금연	kum-yon
non-smoking compartment	금연차	kumyon ch'a
noodles	국수	kuk-soo
north	북	puk
Northern Ireland	북아일랜드	puk a-il-len-du
note (banknote)	지폐	chi-pe
note (letter)	메모	me-mo
November	십일월	ship-il-wol

English	Korean	Romanization
now	지금	chigum
nowadays	요즘	yojum
number (of)	수	soo
number (1, 2, 3, etc.)	숫자	soo-ccha
nurse	간호사	kanhosa

O

object (thing)	물건	mulgon
October	시월	shiwol
octopus	문어	mun-o
of (possessive)	…의	…e

English – Korean

English – Korean

off (light)	꺼졌어요 (꺼지다)	kko-jyossoyo (dic. kkojida)	**how old are you?**	몇살이에요? myo-ssari-yeyo?
(food)	상했어요 (상하다)	sanghessoyo (dic. sanghada)	**olive**	올리브 olli-bu
office	사무실	samushil	**on** (light)	켜졌어요 (켜지다) k'yojyossoyo (dic. k'yojida)
often	자주	chaju	**on the table**	테이블 위에 t'e-i-bul wi-e
oil	기름	kirum	**one** (adj)	하나 hana
oil filter	오일 필터	o-il p'il-t'o	(n)	일 il
OK	좋아요	choayo	**one-way ticket**	편도 티켓 p'yondo t'i-k'et
I'm OK, it's OK	괜찮아요	kwen-ch'a-nayo	**onion**	양파 yang-p'a
OK, let's do that	좋아요, 그렇게 choayo, kurok'e	**to open**	열어요 (열리다) yol-lyoyo (dic. yol-lida)
old	함지다 오래된	hapshida ore twen	**the shop is open**	영업중 yong-op-chung

English	Korean	Romanization
the door is open	문이 열렸어요	muni yol-lyossoyo
operation (medical)	수술	soo-sool
opposite	반대	pande
optician	인과	an-kwa
orange (colour)	오렌지 색	orenji sek
orange (fruit)	오렌지	orenji
orange juice	오렌지 쥬스	orenji ju-su
out	바깥	pa-kkat
out of order	고장	kojang
he's out	외출중이에요	we-ch'ul chung-ieyo
outdoor (pool, etc.)	아외	ya-we

English	Korean	Romanization
oven	오븐	o-bun
overnight train	야행열차	yaheng.yolch'a
oysters	굴	kool
P		
Pacific Ocean	태평양	t'e-p'yong-yang
packet	소포	so-p'o
painful	아파요	ap'ayo
	(아프다)	(dic. ap'uda)
painkiller	진통제	chin-t'ong-je
painting	그림	kurim
oil painting	유화	yu-hwa
palace	궁전	koong-jon
pants (trousers) (men's underwear)	바지	paji
	내복	nebok

English – Korean

paper	종이	chong-i
paper handkerchief	티슈	t'i-syu
paper towels	종이 수건	chong-i soo-gon
Pardon?	네?	ne?
I beg your pardon!	네!	ne!
(didn't hear/ understand)	다시 한번 말씀해 주세요	tashi hanbon malssum hae chuseyo
parents	부모	pumo
your parents	부모님	pumo-nim
park (garden)	공원	kong-won
parking lot	주차장	chuch'a-jang

partner (wife, husband)	배우자 (부인, 남편)	pe-oo-ja (poo-in, namp'yon)
party (evening) (group)	파티	p'a-t'i
pass (permit)	일행	il-heng
passenger	(허가)증	(hoga)chung
passport	승객	sung-gek
passport control	여권	yo-kwon
path	출입국관리소	ch'u-rip-kuk kwal-li-so
to pay	길	kil
	(돈) 내요 / 지불해요	(ton) nae-yo/ chibul haeyo
	(내다) / 지불하다)	(dic. naeda/ chibul hada)
payment	지불	chibul

payphone	공중전화	kong-joong chonhwa		pepper (spice)	후주	hoo-ch'oo
				(vegetable)	피망	p'i-mang
peach	복숭아	pok-soong-a		per...	...에	...e
pear	배	pae		per hour	한 시간에	han shigan-e
pearl	진주	chin-joo		per person	한 사람에	han saram-e
pedestrian (person)	보행자	pohengja		percent	퍼센트	p'o-sen-t'u
				perfume	향수	hyang-soo
pedestrian crossing	횡단보도	hwaeng-dan podo		period (menstruation)	멘스 / 월경	men-su/wol-gyong
pen	볼펜	pol-p'en		person	사람	saram
pencil	연필	yon-p'il		personal organizer	전자 수첩	chonja soo-ch'op
penicillin	페니실린	pe-ni-sil-lin		petrol	기름	kirum
pensioner	연금수령자	yongum suryong-ja		petrol station	주유소	chu-yu-so
people	사람들	saram-dul		pharmacy	약국	yak-kuk

phone	전화	chon-hwa	
to phone	전화해요	chonhwa haeyo	
	(전화하다)	(dic. chonhwa hada)	
phone box	전화박스	chonhwa pak-su	
phone number	전화번호	chonhwa ponho	
phonecard	전화카드	chonhwa k'a-du	
photocopy	복사기	poksagi	
to photocopy	복사해요	poksa haeyo	
	(복사하다)	(dic. poksa hada)	
photograph	사진	sajin	
to photograph	사진을 찍어요	sajin-ul cchi-goyo	
	(사진을	(dic. sajin-ul	
	찍다)	cchik-ta)	

pig	돼지	tweji	
pillow	베개	pege	
pineapple	파인애플	pa-in-e-p'ul	
plan (of a building)	도면	tomyon	
to plan	계획해요	kehwek haeyo	
	(계획하다)	(dic. kehwek hada)	
plane (aircraft)	비행기	piheng-gi	
plaster (sticking plaster)	일회용 반창고	il-hweyong pan-ch'ang-go	
plastic bag	플라스틱 가방	p'ul-la-su-t'ik kabang	
platform (railway)	플랫폼	p'ul-let-p'om	

English	Korean		English	Korean
play (theatre)	연극	yon-guk	post code	우편 번호	up'yon ponho
plug (electrical)	플러그	p'ul-lo-gu	post office	우체국	oo-ch'e-guk
plug socket	콘센트	k'on-sen-t'u	potato	감자	kam-ja
plum	자두	chadoo	pound	파운드	p'a-un-d'u
plumber	배관공	pe-gwan-gong	power cut	정전	chong-jon
p.m. (afternoon)	오후	o-hoo	power point	콘센트	k'on-sen-t'u
poisonous	유독성	yu-dok-song	prawn	새우	se-oo
police	경찰	kyongch'al	pregnant	임신	imshin
police station	경찰서	kyongch'al-so	prescription	처방전	ch'obang-jon
policeman	경찰관	kyongch'al-gwan	present	선물	sonmul
pool (swimming)	수영장	soo-yong-jang	president (of a company)	사장	sajang
pork	돼지 고기	twejî kogi	pretty	예쁜	ye-ppun
portion (of food)	일인분	i-rin-bun	price	값/가격	kap/kagyok
postcard	엽서	yop-so			

English – Korean

English – Korean

priest		
(Buddhist)	중/승려	choong/sung-nyo
(Catholic)	신부	shimbu
(Protestant)	목사	moksa
prince	왕자	wangja
princess	공주	kongju
private	개인	ke-in
prize	상	sang
problem	문제	munje
there's a problem	문제가 있어요	munje-ga issoyo
programme (TV, etc.)	프로그램	p'u-ro-gu-rem
(computer)	프로그램	p'u-ro-gu-rem
promise	약속	yak-sok

it's a promise	약속이에요	yaksok-iyeyo
to pronounce	발음해요	parum haeyo
	(발음하다)	(dic. parum hada)
how is it pronounced?	어떻게 발음해요?	ottok'e parum haeyo?
Protestant	개신교	kae-shin-gyo
public holiday	공휴일	kong-hyuil
public toilet	공중변소	kongjung pyonso
to pull	당기세요	tangiseyo
	(당기다)	(dic. tangida)
puncture	펑크	p'ong-k'u
purse	지갑	chigap

English	Korean	Romanization
push	미세요	miseyo
	(밀다)	(dic. milda)
pushchair	유모차	yumoch'a
Q		
qualification	자격	chagyok
quality	질 / 품질	chil/p'umjil
queen	여왕	yo-wang
question (n)	질문	chilmun
queue	줄	chool
quickly	빨리	ppal-li
quiet (place)	조용한	choyonghan

English	Korean	Romanization
R		
rabies	광견병	kwang-gyon-pyong
race (sport)	경기	kyung-gi
race (people)	인종	in-jong
radio	라디오	ra-di-o
railway station	(기차) 역	yok
rain	비	pi
it's raining	비가 와요	piga wayo
	드물어요	tumuroyo
rare (unique)	(드물다)	(dic. tumulda)
(food)	레어	re-o
rash (skin)	발진	palchin
raw	생	saeng
razor	레이저	re-i-jo

English – Korean

English – Korean

razor blades	면도날	myon-do-nal
ready	준비	chumbi
receipt	영수증	yong-soo-jung
reception (desk)	리셉션	ri-sep-syon
receptionist	데스크	de-su-k'u
recipe	안내원	annewon
to recommend	요리법	yori-pop
	추천해요	ch'u-ch'on haeyo
	(추천하다)	(dic. ch'uch'on hada)
what do you recommend?	추천해 주세요?	ch'uch'on hae chuseyo?
record (music, etc.)	음반	umban

red (n)	적색	chok-sek
(adj)	빨간	ppalgan
reduction (for student, etc.)	할인	hal-in
refreshments	음료수	umnyosoo
refund	환불	hwanbul
I'd like a refund	환불해 주세요	hwanbul hae chuseyo
region	지역	chiyok
to reimburse	환급해요	hwangup haeyo
	(환급하다)	(dic. hwangup hada)
relative (family member)	친척	ch'in-ch'ok

relatively (comparitively)	비 교 적	pigyo-jok		repeat	반 복 해 요 (반 복 하다)	panbok haeyo (dic. panbok hada)
reliable (person)	믿 을 만 해 요	midul man haeyo		can you repeat that, please?	다시 한번 말씀 해 주세요 ?	tashi hanbon malssum hae chuseyo?
religion	종 교	chong-gyo		reservation	예 약	yeyak
to rent	렌 트 해 요 (렌트하다)	ren-t'u haeyo (dic. ren-t'u hada)		reserved seat	지 정 석	chijong-sok
rent (for house, flat)	렌 트	ren-t'u		resort (seaside)	휴 양 지	hyuyangji
				rest (relaxation)	휴 식	hyushik
to repair	수 리 해 요 (수리하다) / 고 쳐 요 (고치다)	soo-ri haeyo (dic. soori hada)/ koch'yoyo (dic. koch'ida)		to rest	쉬 어 요 (쉬 다)	swi-oyo (dic. swida)
				restaurant	식 당	shik-tang
				restaurant car	식 당 차	shiktang-ch'a

English – Korean

English – Korean

retire	은퇴해요 (은퇴하다)	unt'we haeyo (dic. unt'we hada)
to return (to go back) (to give back)	돌아가요 (돌아가다) 돌려줘요 (돌려주다)	tora kayo (dic. tora kada) tollyo-jwoyo (dic. tollyo-juda)
(to return a purchase)	반품해요 (반품하다)	panp'um haeyo (dic. panp'um hada)
return ticket	왕복표	wangbok-p'yo
reverse-charge call	콜렉트 콜	kol-lek-t'u k'ol
rheumatism	류마티즘	ryumat'ijum

rice (cooked)	쌀 밥	ssal pap
right (correct)	맞아요 (맞다)	majayo (dic. matta)
on/to the right	오른쪽에	orun cchoʻge
ring (for finger)	반지	panji
river	강	kang
road	길 / 도로	kil/toro
road sign	도로표지	toro p'yoji
to roast, bake or grill	구워요 (굽다)	kuwoyo (dic. kup-ta)
room (in house, hotel)	방	pang
(space)	공간	kong-gan

it takes up	공간을 차지해요	kongggan-ul ch'aji haeyo
room	룸	rum
room service	룸서비스	rum so-bi-su
rotten (meat, fruit)	상했어요	sang-hessoyo
route	루트 / 길	ru-t'u/kil
row (theatre, etc.)	열	yol
royal	왕실의	wangshi-re
rubbish (nonsense)	쓰레기	ssuregi
rucksack	어뜨리	ong-t'ori
	배낭	penang
rush hour	출퇴근 시간	ch'u-t'we-gun shigan

S

safe (adj)	안전한	anjon-han
safety belt	안전벨트	anjon belt'u
sailing (sport)	세일링	se-il-ling
salad	샐러드 / 야채	sel-lo-du/yach'e
salary	월급	wolgup
sale (in shops)	세일	se-il
salesman	세일즈맨	se-il-ju men
(in store)	판매원	p'an mewon
salmon	연어	yono
salt	소금	sogum
sandals	샌들	sen-dul
sandwich	샌드위치	sen-du-wi-ch'i
sardine	정어리	chong-o-ri

English – Korean

satellite channels	위성방송	wisong pangsong	Scotland	스코틀랜드	su-k'o-t'ul-len-du
Saturday	토요일	t'oyoil	Scottish (person)	스코틀랜드 사람	su-k'o-t'ul-len-du saram
sauce	소스/간장	sosu/kanjang	screw (n)	나사 (못)	nasa (mot)
to save (life)	구해요 (구하다)	kuheyo (dic. kuhada)	screwdriver	드라이버	tu-ra-i-bo
(money)	저금해요	chogum haeyo (dic. chogum hada)	scuba diving	스쿠버 다이빙	su-k'u-bo-da-i-bing
			sculpture (object)	조각	chogak
to say	말해요 (말하다)	mal haeyo (dic. malhada)	sea	바다	pada
scenery	경치	kyongch'i	sea sickness	배 멀미	pemolmi
school	학교	hakkyo	seafood	해산물	hesanmul
scissors	가위	kawi	seaside	해변	hebyon
			at the seaside	해변에서	hebyon-eso

English	Korean	
season (of year)	계절	kejol
season ticket	정기권	chong-gi-kwon
seat	자리 / ~석	chari/sok
seat belt	안전벨트	anjon-belt'u
seaweed	해조 / 미역	hech'o/miyok
secretary	비서	piso
security guard	경비원	kyongbiwon
to see	봐요 (보다)	pwayo (dic. poda)
self-catering	셀프	sel-p'u
self-service	케이터링	k'ei-t'o-ring
	셀프 서비스	sel-p'u so-bi-su
to sell	팔아요	p'arayo
	(팔다)	(dic. p'alda)
sellotape®	스카치	su-k'a-ch'i-
	테이프	t'e-i-p'u
to send	보내요	poneyo
	(보내다)	(dic. poneda)
to send	를 보내요	...ul poneyo
someone off		
senior citizen	노인	noin
September	구월	ku-wol
service (in	서비스	so-bi-su
restaurant, etc.)		
service charge	봉사료	pong-sa-ryo
set menu	세트 메뉴	se-t'u menyu
sex	성	song
shampoo	샴푸	sham-p'u
to share	분담해요	bundam haeyo
	(분담하다)	(dic. bundam hada)

English – Korean

English – Korean

English	Korean	Romanization
shares (stocks)	주식	chushik
to shave	면도해요 (면도하다)	myondo haeyo (dic. myondo hada)
shaving cream	면도 크림	myondo k'u-rim
sheet	시이트	shi-i-t'u
shellfish	조개 / 갑각류	choge/ kapkak-nyu
ship	배	pae
shirt	셔츠	shyo-ch'u
shoe	구두	kudu
shoe polish	구두약	kudu-yak
shop	가게	kage
shopping	쇼핑	shyo-p'ing
to go shopping	쇼핑해요 (쇼핑하다)	shyo-p'ing haeyo (dic. shyo-p'ing hada)
shopping trolley	쇼핑 트롤리	shyo-p'ing t'u-rol-li
short cut	지름길	chirum-kil
shorts	반바지	pan-baji
shoulder	어깨	okke
show (at theatre, etc.)	쇼 / 공연	shyo/kong-yon
shower	샤워	shya-wo
shrimps	새우	se-oo
to shut	닫아요 (닫다)	tadayo (dic. tat-ta)
sick (ill)	뼝	pyong

English			
to be sick	토해요	t'ohaeyo	
(vomit)	(토하다)	(dic. t'ohada)	
sightseeing	관광	kwan-gwang	
signature	서명 / 사인	somyong/sa-in	
silk	비단 / 실크	pidan/silku	
silver	은	un	
single (person)	독신 / 싱글	tok-shin/singul	
(bed, room)	일인용	irin-yong	
(ticket)	편도	p'yondo	
sink	싱크 / 세면대	sing-k'u/ semyonde	
(bathroom, etc.)			
sister (younger)	여동생	yodongseng	
(older)	누나 / 언니	nuna/onni	
size	크기	k'u-gi	
(clothes)	사이즈 / 치수	sa-riju/ch'isoo	

to ski	스키 타요	su-k'i tayo (dic.	
	(스키타다)	su-k'i-hada)	
ski boots	스키 부츠	su-k'i-boo-ch'u	
ski pass	리프트 권	li-p'u-t'u kwon	
skirt	치마	ch'ima	
to sleep	자요 (자다)	chayo (dic. chada)	
sleeping bag	침낭	ch'imnang	
sleeping pill	수면제	soo-myonje	
slippers	슬리퍼	sul-li-p'o	
slow	늦은	nujun	
small (n)	작은	chagun	
smell (n)	냄새	nemsae	
to smoke	담배 피워요	tambe p'iwoyo	
	(담배	(dic. tambe	
	피우다)	p'i-uda)	

smoking	흡연	hup-yon
no smoking	금연	kum-yon
snack	간식	kanshik
snow (n)	눈	noon
it's snowing	눈이 와요	noon-i wayo
soap	비누	pinoo
soap powder	가루 비누	karu pinoo
sober (not drunk)	안 취한	an ch'wi-han
sock	양말	yangmal
soda water	소다수	soda-soo
soft drink	음료수	umnyo-soo
something	어떤 것	otton kot
sometimes	가끔	kakkum
son	아들	adul
song	노래	norae

soon	곧	kot
sore head	두통	tu-t'ong
sore throat	목이 아파요	mogi ap'ayo
sorry	미안합니다	mianhamnida
I'm sorry	미안합니다	mianhamnida
soup	국/스프	kuk/su-p'u
south	남	nam
South Africa	남아프리카	nam ap'u-ri-k'a
South African	남아프리카	nam ap'u-
(person)	사람	ri-k'a saram
souvenir	기념품	kinyom-p'um
soya sauce	간장	kanjang
spanner	스패너	su-p'e-no
to speak	말해요	mal-haeyo (dic.
	(말하다)	mal-hada)

do you speak English?	영어 (를) 하세요?	yong-o (mal)haseyo?	
speciality	전문	chonmun	
speed limit	속도 제한	sok-to chehan	
to spell	써요 (쓰다)	ssoyo (dic. ssu-da)	
how is it spelt?	어떻게 써요?	ottok'e ssoyo?	
to spend (money)	(돈을) 써요 (돈을) 쓰다)	(ton-ul) ssoyo ((dic. (ton-ul) sssuda)	
spicy	매운	mae-un	
spirits (alcohol)	양주/독주	yang-joo	
	숟가락	sut-karak	
	스포츠/ 운동	su-p'o-ch'u/ undong	

sprain (ankle, etc.)	삐었어요 (삐다)	ppi-ossoyo (dic. ppida)	
spring (season)	봄	pom	
hot spring	온천	onch'on	
squash (game, drink)	스쿼시	su-k'wo-shi	
squid	오징어	ojing-o	
stadium	경기장	kyong-gi-jang	
stamps (for letters)	우표	oo-p'yo	
star (in sky)	별	pyol	
(in film)	스타	su-t'a	
station	역	yok	
stationer's	문방구	munbang-gu	
statue	동상	tongsang	

English – Korean

English – Korean

English	Korean	Romanization
eak	스테이크,	su-t'e-i-k'u
eep	험한,	homhan
stereo	가파른, 스테레오	kaparun, su-t'e-re-o
stomach	배	pae
stomach ache	복통	pok-t'ong
storm	강풍	kang-p'ung
straight on	똑바로	ttok-pparo
strange (odd)	이상한	isanghan
strawberry	딸기	ttalgi
street	길/도로	kil/toro
string (for wrapping)	끈	kkun
strong (person)	힘센	him-sen
strong (material)	튼튼한	t'un-t'un-han

English	Korean	Romanization
stuck (jammed)	붙어 있어요 (붙어 있다)	put'o issoyo (dic. put'oitta)
student	학생	hakseng
suburbs	교외	kyo-we
subway (metro)	지하철	chihach'ol
suddenly	갑자기	kapchagi
sugar	설탕	solt'ang
sugar-free	무가당	mugadang
suit	슈트/한벌	syu-t'u/hanpol
suitcase	슈트케이스	syu-t'u k'e-i-su
summer	여름	yorum
sun	태양	t'e-yang
to sunbathe	일광욕해요 (일광욕하다)	ilgwangyok haeyo (dic. ilgwangyok hada)

suntan	썬 탠	sŏn-t'en	to swim	수영해요	suyong-haeyo	suyong-haeyo
Sunday	일요일	iryoil		(수영하다)	(dic. suyong	(dic. suyong
sunglasses	썬글라스	sŏn-gŭl-la-su			hada)	hada)
sunstroke	일사병	ilsa-pyong	swimsuit	수영복	suyong-bok	suyong-bok
supermarket	수퍼마켓	su-p'o-ma-k'et	to switch off	꺼요 (끄다)	kkoyo (dic. kkuda)	kkoyo (dic. kkuda)
supper (dinner)	저녁	chonyok	to switch on	켜요 (켜다)	k'yoyo (k'yoda)	k'yoyo (k'yoda)
surgery	진찰실	chin-ch'al-shil	synagogue	유대교회	yudae-kyohwe	yudae-kyohwe
(of doctor)						
surname	성	song	**T**			
sweet	단	tan	table	테이블	t'e-i-bul	t'e-i-bul
(not savoury)			to take	걸려요	kol-lyoyo	kol-lyoyo
sweetener	감미료	kamminyo		(걸리다)	(dic. kollida)	(dic. kollida)
sweets	사탕	sat'ang	how long	얼마나	olmana	olmana
			does it take?	걸려요?	kollyoyo?	kollyoyo?

English – Korean

English	Korean	Romanization
to talk	애기 해요 (애기 하다)	yegi-haeyo (dic. yegi ahda)
tampon	탐폰	tampon
tap	마개 / 꼭지	mage/kkokchi
tape (sticky)	스카치	su-k'a-ch'i
(audio)	테이프	t'e-i-p'u
	카세트	k'a-se-t'u
	테이프	t'e-i-p'u
to taste (of something)	맛있어요 (맛있다)	masissoyo (dic. masitta)
to taste (something)	맛을 봐요 (맛을 보다)	masul pwayo (dic. masul poda)
tax	세금	segum
tax-free	면세	myonse
taxi	택시	t'ek-shi
by taxi	택시로	t'ek-shi-ro
taxi driver	택시 운전수	t'ek-shi-unjonsoo
taxi rank	택시 승차장	t'ek-shi sungch'ajang
tea (green)	녹차	nok-ch'a
(English)	홍차	hongch'a
teacher	선생님	sonsaengnim
teeth	이 / 지 아	i/ch'a
telephone (n)	전화	chonhwa
telephone box	전화 박스	chonhwa bak-su
telephone directory	전화번호부	chonhwa ponhobu
telephone number	전화번호	chonhwa ponho
television	테레비전	t'e-re-bi-jon

English	Korean		
to tell	말해요 (dic. 말하다)	mal haeyo (dic. mal hada)	
temperature	온도 / 열	ondo/yol	
I have a temperature	열이 있어요	yori issoyo	
temple	절	chol	
tennis	테니스	t'e-ni-su	
tennis court	테니스 코트	t'e-ni-su k'o-t'u	
tennis racket	테니스 라켓	t'e-ni-su-ra-k'et	
tent	텐트	t'en-t'u	
terminal (airport)	터미널	t'e-mi-nal	
thank you	감사합니다 / 고맙습니다	kamsahamnida/ komapsumnida	
thank you	감사합니다 / 고맙습니다	(정 말) kamsahamnida/ komapsumnida	(chongmal)
very much			
that one (near the listener)	그거	kugo	
(away from the listener and speaker)	저 거	chogo	
theatre	극장	kuk-chang	
thermometer	온도계	ondoge	
thick (paper, board)	두꺼운	tukko-un	
(rope, cord)	굵은	kulgun	
(sauce)	진한	chinhan	
thief	도둑	toduk	

English – Korean   240 | 241

English – Korean

thin	얇은	yalbun	**ticket office**	매표소	mep'yoso
(paper, sauce)			**ticket vending**	자동 판매기	chadong
(rope, cord)	가는	kanun	**machine**		p'anmegi
thing	물건	mulgon	**tight**	촘촘한	ch'om-
my things	내 것	ne got			ch'omhan
thirsty	목말라요	mok mallayo	**tights**	타이츠	t'a·i·su
	(목 마르다)	(dic. mok	**time**	시간	shigan
		maruda)	*this time*	이번에	ibone
I'm thirsty	목말라요	mok mallayo	*what time is it?*	몇 시에요?	myossi·yeyo?
this one	이거	igo	**timetable**	시간표	shiganp'yo
throat	목	mok	(train, etc.)		
thunder	천둥	ch'ondung	**tin opener**	깡통 따개	kkangt'ong
thunderstorm	우뢰와 폭우	ure wa pokwoo			tta·ge
Thursday	목요일	mog·yoil	**tinned**	통조림	t'ongjorim
ticket	표	p'yo	**tinfoil**	일미늄 호일	al·mi·nyum hoil

tired	피곤해요 (피곤하다)	p'igon haeyo (dic. p'igon hada)
I'm tired	피곤해요	p'igon haeyo
tissue	티슈	t'i-syu
toast	토스트	t'o-su-t'u
tobacconist's	담배 가게	tambe kage
today	오늘	onul
tofu	두부	tubu
toilet (informal)	변소	pyonso
(polite)	화장실	hwajangshil
toilet paper	휴지	hyuji
toiletries	화장품	hwajangp'um
toll	통행료	t'ongheng-nyo
tomato	토마토	t'o-ma-t'o
tomorrow	내일	ne-il

tomorrow	내일 오후	neil o-hoo
afternoon	내일 아침	neil ach'im
tomorrow morning		
tomorrow night	내일 밤	neil pam
tonight	오늘 밤	onul pam
tooth	이/지아	i/ch'ia
toothache	치통	ch'it'ong
toothbrush	치솔	ch'i-sol
toothpaste	치약	ch'i-yak
torch	손전등/후레쉬	sonjondung/ huraeshi
tough (meat)	질긴	chilgin
tour (sightseeing)	투어/여행	t'u-o/yoheng

English – Korean

English – Korean

English	Korean	
tourist	관광객	kwangwang-gek
tourist office	관광 안내소	kwangwang anneso
towel	수건	sugon
town	마을 / 도시	maul/toshi
town centre	시내	shi-ne
town plan	도시 계획	toshi ke-hwek
toy	장난감	changnan-gam
tracksuit	운동복	oondong-bok
tradition	전통	chont'ong
traffic	교통	kyot'ong
traffic jam	교통체증	kyot'ong ch'ejung
traffic lights	신호등	shinhodung

English	Korean	
train	기차	kich'a
translation	번역	ponyok
translator	번역가	ponyok-ka
to travel	여행해요	yoheng haeyo
	(여행하다)	(dic. yoheng hada)
travel agent's	여행사	yohengsa
traveller's cheque	여행자 수표	yohengja soop'yo
tree	나무	namu
trip	여행	yoheng
trousers	바지	paji
trout	송어	song-o
true (real)	정말	chongmal
Tuesday	화요일	hwa-yoil

tuna	참치	ch'amch'i
to turn off (light, etc.)	꺼요 (끄다)	kkoyo (dic. kkuda)
to turn on (light, etc.)	켜요 (켜다)	k'yoyo (k'yoda)
tweezers	족집게, 핀셋	chok-chip-ke, pinsetu
twin-bedded room	트윈 베드룸	t'u-win be-du-rum
tyre	타이어	t'a-i-o

U

ulcer	궤양	kwe-yang
umbrella	우산	usan
uncle	아저씨	ajossi

underground (metro)	지하철	chihach'ol
to understand	알아요 (알다)	arayo (dic. alda)
I don't understand	모르겠어요	morugessoyo
do you understand?	알겠어요?	algessoyo?
underwear	내복	nebok
unemployed	무직	mujik
United Kingdom	영국	yong-guk
United States of America	미국	miguk
university	대학교	tehakkyo

244|245

English – Korean

to unpack	풀어요	p'uroyo
(case)	(풀다)	(dic. p'ulda)
urgent	긴박한 / 급한	kinbak'an/kup'an
V		
vacancy	빈 방	pin pang
(in hotel)		
vaccination	예방주사	yebang chusa
valid	유효한	yuhyohan
(passport, etc.)		
valuables	귀중품	kwijungp'um
van	벤/트럭	ben/t'u-rok
vase	꽃병	kkot-pyong
VAT	부가가치세	puga-gach'ise
vegetable	야채	yach'e

vegetarian	채식주의자	ch'eshik chuija
vehicle	교통수단	kyot'ong sudan
very	아주	aju
video	비디오	pi-di-o
video game	비디오 게임	pi-di-o ge-im
village	마을	maul
vinegar	식초	shik-ch'o
virus	바이러스	pa-i-ro-su
visa	비자	pija
to visit	방문해요	pangmun haeyo
	(방문하다)	(dic. pangmun hada)
visitor	방문객	pangmun-gek
(tourist)	관광객	kwangwang-gek
vitamin	비타민	pi-t'a-min

W

English	Korean	Romanization
wage	임금 / 월급	imgum/wolgup
waist	허리	hori
to wait for...	...을 기다려요 (기다리다)	...ul kidaryoyo (dic. kidarida)
waiter	웨이터	we-i-t'o
waiting room	대기실 / 대합실	tegishil/ tehapshil
waitress	웨이트리스	we-i-t'u-ri-su
wake up	일어나요 (일어나다)	ironayo (dic. ironada)
Wales	웨일즈	we-il-ju
walk	걸어가요 (걸어가다)	korogayo (dic. korogada)

English	Korean	Romanization
to go for a walk	산책해요/ 산보해요 (산책/산보 하다)	sanch'ek haeyo/ sampo haeyo (dic. sanch'ek/ sampo hada)
wallet	지갑	chigap
to want	...하고 싶어요	...hago ship'oyo
wardrobe	옷장	otchang
warm	따뜻한	tta-ttu-t'an
to wash	씻어요 (씻다)	ssisoyo (dic. ssitta)
washing machine	세탁기	set'akki
washing-up liquid	세제	seje

English – Korean

English	Korean	Romanization	English	Korean	Romanization
washing powder	가루비누	karu pinu	way out	출구	ch'ulgu
wasp	말벌	malbol	we	우리	oori
watch (on wrist)	(손목) 시계	(sonmok) shige	weak (physically)	약한	yak'an
to watch TV	티비를 봐요 (보다)	t'i-bi-rul pwayo (dic. poda)	weak (tea, etc.)	묽은	mulgun
water	물	mool	weather	날씨	nalssi
hot water	온수 / 뜨거운 물	onsoo/ttugoun mool	weather forecast	일기 예보	ilgi yebo
			website	웹사이트	wep-sa-i-t'u
water skiing	수상 스키	soosang su-ki	wedding	결혼식	kyolhonshik
watermelon	수박	soobak	Wednesday	수요일	soo-yoil
waterproof	방수	pangsoo	week	주	chu
way (manner)	방법	pangbop	weekday	평일	p'yong-il
way (route)	방향	panghyang	weekend	주말	chumal
way in	입구	ip-ku	weekly	매주	meju
			weight	무게	muge

English	Korean		English	Korean
well	잘	chal	whisky	위스키 / 양주	wi-su-ki/yangju
well done	잘 했어요	chal hessoyo	white (n)	빼 색	peksek
I am well	좋아요	choayo	(adj)	흰	hin
Welsh (person)	웨일즈 사람	we-il-ju saram	who	누구	nugu
west (n)	서	so	whose	누구의	nugu-e
(adj)	서쪽의	so-ccho-ge	whose is it?	누구 거예요?	nugu go-eyo?
wet	축축한	ch'uk-ch'uk'an	why	왜	we
what	뭐	mwo	wide	넓은	nolbun
what is it?	그게 뭐예요?	kuge mwo-eyo?	widow	미망인	mimang-in
wheel (of car)	바퀴	pak'wi	wife (own)	아내 / 집사람	ane/chipsaram
wheelchair	휠체어	hwil-ch'e-o	(somebody else's)	부인	puin
when	언제	onje?	to win	이겨요	igyoyo (dic. igida)
where	어디	odi?		(이기다)	
which	어느 거	onu go	wind (air)	바람	param
which is it?	어느 거예요?	onu go-eyo?	window	창문	ch'angmun

English – Korean

English - Korean

English	Korean	Romanization	English	Korean	Romanization
windscreen	차 앞유리	ch'a amnyuri	wool	모직 / 울	mojik/ool
windscreen	와이퍼	wa-i-p'o	word	단어	tano
wipers			to work (person)	일해요	il haeyo
windsurfing	윈드 서핑	win-du-so-p'ing			(dic. ilhada)
wine	와인 / 포도주	wa-in/p'odoju	(machine, car)	작동해요	chaktong haeyo
red wine	레드 와인 /	redu wain/		(작동하다)	(dic. chaktong
	적포도주	chok p'odoju			hada)
white wine	화이트 와인 /	hwaitu wain/	world	세계	sege
	배포도주	pek p'odoju	wrist	손목	sonmok
wine list	와인 리스트	wa-in-li-su-t'u	to write	써요 (쓰다)	ssoyo (dic. ssuda)
winter	겨울	kyo-ul	writer (author)	작자 / 작가	choja/chakka
with (a person)	...하고	...hago	wrong	틀린, 나쁜	tullin, nappun
woman	여자	yoja	**X**		
wonderful	훌륭한	hul-lyunghan	x-ray	엑스 레이	ek-su-re-i
wood	나무	namu			

Y

year	년	nyon
for one year	일년간	ilnyon-gan
one year old	한 살	han sal
five years old	다섯 살	tasot sal
next year	내년	nenyon
last year	작년	chang-nyon
yellow (n)	노란색	noransek
(adj)	노란색의	noranse-ge
yes	네	ne
yes, please	네, 부탁합니다	ne, put'ak' amnida
yesterday	어제	oje
yet	아직	ajik

not yet

not yet	아직 안 됐어요	ajik an twessoyo
youth hostel	유스호스텔	yu-su-ho-su-t'el

Z

zebra crossing	횡단보도	hwengdan podo
zero	영 / 제로	yong/chero
zip	자크 / 지프	chak'u/chip'u
zone	지대	chide
zoo	동물원	tongmool-won

Further titles in Collins' phrasebook range
Collins Gem Phrasebook

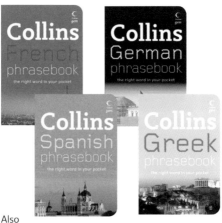

Also

available as **Phrasebook CD Pack**

Other titles in the series

Arabic	Greek	Polish
Cantonese	Italian	Portuguese
Croatian	Japanese	Russian
Czech	Korean	Spanish
Dutch	Latin American	Thai
French	Spanish	Turkish
German	Mandarin	Vietnamese

Collins Easy: Photo Phrasebook

Also available as
**Phrasebook
CD Pack**

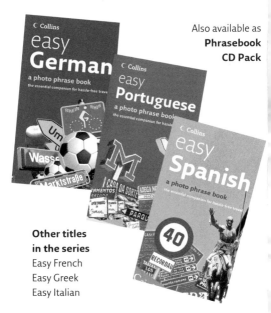

**Other titles
in the series**
Easy French
Easy Greek
Easy Italian

Collins Phrasebook & Dictionary

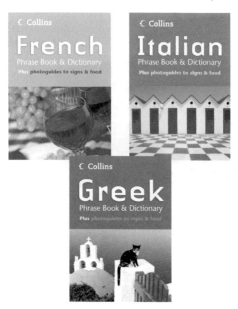

Also available as **Phrasebook CD Pack**
Other titles in the series
German Japanese Portuguese Spanish